CONFESSIONS OF A CAR ADDICT
…and other musings!

Written and Illustrated By
RODGER J. PIERSANT

Dedicated to my Mom!
In loving memory of Dad.

TABLE OF CONTENTS

PREFACE

The Automobile has been one of man's greatest and most enduring innovations. Although cars have become commonplace in living a cosmopolitan life, many still have the ability to produce endorphins by the millions when ex-ercising their limits or beholding their beauty.  From the designer's drawing board to the owner's garage, cars capture our imagination like no other accessory. Beginning with the selling of the first production vehicles by Karl Benz in 1886, automobiles have been an ever-evolving con-venience made by people bent on improved mechanics while attempting to out-maneuver our forever chang-ing sense of fashion. A muscular running horse in the nose of a Mustang, or the gills of a shark on the side of a Vette affirm the maker's psychology in creating desirable vehicles, alive with personality. And often the final de-tail differentiating the most beautiful and powerful from the pedestrian and mundane of the species, is a number above or below three-hundred!

If the car was some inert object, some window dressing or a picture hanging on the wall, our enthusiasm for them might be muted. But these accessories come to life with the turn of a key. Time and again, we perform complex coordination of skill, judgment, and finesse, propelling our cars along vast super highways, tossing them back and forth on twisty back roads, or whipping them around race tracks found in hamlets throughout the world. For the enthusiast, every drive promises to be an adventure! Once we have experienced the rush of adrenaline from a high speed run in a radical machine, we live for the moment to strap in and do it again! And as if to foil the designers' hard work and prove we owners always want our way, we use our creativity to change the automobile's color, swap out its wheels, or add a horsepower chip to further challenge the science of physics so thoroughly considered by a legion of engineers before it left the assembly line. Finally, what car fanatic hasn't detailed his ride with hours of loving care, and then stood back, drinking in its freshly finished, deeply waxed beauty in the shade on a cool spring day?

So, while some just see the car as transportation, I see a fascinating, multi-dimensional creation. And as a created thing, every one is an artist's canvas with the giftedness of its creator on display. Furthering the arts, however rudimentary, this book was created *about* cars, framed in my family's memories. Although not the great literary work of a Steinbeck or a Hemingway, it was joyfully penned from my heart for both the amateur and advanced car lovers, and for those who know how oddly diverse my life as been. It was written to bring a smile to the reader, and an occasional head nod when a familiar chord was struck. As I said to my wife, "The odd mix of cars and family memories will make more sense once you read it!"

Incidentally, when you cross a car nut like me with a seminary education, you get a hot-rodder interested in both the material and the spiritual. Guys like us seek and find the beauty behind the complexity of a carburetor, the artistry of a paint job, and the mechanical wizardry to produce a 330 mile per hour quarter mile run. We're all about motivations in life and the condition of the soul behind the machines.

I'm deeply grateful for the love of God and family, and a heritage that has given me the security to quip, muse, and just be my broken self. Come ride with me and see what I mean…

PART ONE
1951 to 1966
If only I could drive!

Chapter One
THE TEST

Are you a car guy? I mean, *really* a car guy (okay or gal)? Here's a test....let's say you and your wife roll up to the light in the family SUV. You glance in the rear view mirror and note a Black '32 Ford Highboy coming from behind. You determine that he'll be idling directly to your left in about six seconds. Five, four, three... your eyes shift to the side mirror as you press the window button down (don't want to be too obvious). He rumbles up and you exchange a knowing look and a nearly imperceptible nod. You sweep your eyes front to rear, registering Halibrand wheels, Coker vintage tires, and know she's all steel by the gloss and depth of the flawless black finish. You swing your head around to your wife, who is shaking her head as if to say, "NO SOUP FOR YOU!" You sigh, shoulders slumping slightly, and your eyes track back to some really well done hood louvers. You can tell by the engine note the guy's running Ford power under the hood, and then you think arrogantly, "That wasn't a guess!" Your left hand involuntarily raises and forms the universal hotrod "thumbs up" gesture, and he, being very hip, subtly flashes it back. The light goes green, and he rewards you with a cool little "chirp and go!" Meanwhile you're still sitting at the light and wifey-poo sarcastically says, "Uh, Mr. Foose? Can WE leave?" Yeah, you're sick, buddy! You've got it real bad.

But you say you're not sure you're hooked? Well, have you ever lost your place in a meaningful conversation while getting a better look at a new ZR1 Vette? Can you instinctively spot a good Cobra replica by its instrumentation and reverse lock-out? Does your spine tingle when you see the numbers "427" together on anything? Do your friends always call YOU when something goes haywire with their car? Or, do you stare when a beautiful two-tone 3000 Healey drives by, remembering when you and your buddy knocked the muffler off turning into a driveway, or enjoyed the naughty pleasure of flipping its sexy O/D switch?

Come on! You're the guy who has six car magazine subscriptions and literally another thousand car mags piled in the basement. You've had to endure the "When-Are-You-Getting-Rid-of-Those-Old-Things!!" speech, am I right? And I bet half of your garage is filled with a totally cool car and enough parts to make another one. Yeah, you're the poor fool who has stored in your brain every Chevy, Ford, and Mopar engine made through four decades, or can tell what engine is in that '62 Impala by the fender flags, true? Yes sir, you're pretty much a goner!

If names like Halibrand, Coker, or Foose don't ring a bell, then I might suggest that the rest of this book will simply confuse you. But if you resonated with anything said, then reading this will most likely make your sickness worse. No, I'm sorry, it WILL make it worse! I can't help you. I can barely help myself.

You see, this book is the result of a terminal condition known as "MAO" (Massive Auto Overload). In my case, it is the accumulation of 59 years of mindless car facts and sensory sheet metal and rubber experiences. The doctor said to just let some of it spill out. It's ugly, but what's an addict to do? And who would understand better than another addict? It's for us guys who have lived with this obscenely expensive habit and have masked it with stupid statements like, "Come on honey... this bulb was only .36 cents!" Or, "But sweetie, you'll look so beautiful riding in it!"

But if you can endure some of the sappy stuff, I've written it as a way to connect to like minded folks while archiving some of my favorite memories. It seems that the automobile was central to hundreds of memorable life events, and this was a fun way to gather what seems to be otherwise quickly evaporating. I have my addiction under some semblance of control, down to one twin turbocharged BMW and three magazine subscriptions. But I could fall off the station wagon anytime and am working my steps with this effort. Lest you think me a sexist pig, I DO realize there are some ladies who have the addiction gene. Forgive me in advance for the male slant of these writings.

So, go ahead and enjoy the ride. There's no stopping you. But, if you don't already have MAO, you will when you've finished reading! You too will be hunting for ways to purge! Please, just try not to buy another car. Write a book instead!

Chapter Two
NEIGHBORS, START YOUR ENGINES!

It was one of those childhood things that just bloomed; from playing with toy cars on my bed with my friend Jimmy, to collecting those very first metal matchbox vehicles in real matchboxes, from carefully gluing and painting AMT models (being sure not to get glue on the windshield), to opening my most desired Christmas gift, a slot car track featuring a red 250 GTO Ferrari and a white Mustang G.T. 350. Or, from fabricating a go-cart out of wood and an old Radio Flyer wagon (we called it the "deathcart"), to having my first real wheels (the "deathcar!") in the driveway, these are the memories of a childhood infatuation, generously mixed with life, and relived on these pages.

My fascination with the car grew into a considerable passion, largely fostered by a six year older brother, Doug, who was more crazed and eaten up than I. He was like standing in front of open nuclear rods…I couldn't help but mutate! Whenever I wasn't thinking about cars, he was, so there was hardly a moment when one of us wasn't reminding the other of some cool car or scene we'd just experienced. So, this is my life, remembered in stories about the automobile, which acted as pencil marks on the wall, scored by Mom to confirm my last growth spurt and best told in living color about a boy and a family obsessed with one thing… the car!

I'm from a working, middle class tribe, who lived on the edge of Baltimore city in a precinct called

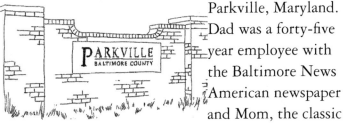

Parkville, Maryland. Dad was a forty-five year employee with the Baltimore News American newspaper and Mom, the classic stay-at-home "house wife" until I was nine. My older brother and I were separated by a sister, Cheryl (for whom we perfected the art of teasing), and, overall, we were a pretty normal 1950's family. Yes, we had a few bruises and bumps, but we survived intact and lived to tell some pretty hilarious stories.

The central players in my life were my family and my best buddies, Jimmy, Buddy and Gary, most of whom lived within yards of me. Our neighbors and the safety of the neighborhood shaped me far more than I will be able to explain here. There were eighteen boys (and a couple of adorable girls) living in the eleven houses surrounding us. Sprinkle in liberally our collective fanaticism for the Colts and Orioles, the presence of my elementary school (literally next to our house), the influence of our church (one block away), the love for our bicycles (complete with the baseball cards clothes pinned to the fork), our modest, individual homes and our glorious cars, and you had the world in which I lived.

Like most kids, my 20" bike repainted four or five times, was my trusty steed, and I explored the far reaches of Parkville, always without fear and half remembering the rule to come home when the street lights came on. We lived on Willoughby Road, a straight, house-lined, two-mile-long side street, which ran east and west and was accessed by the main north-south thoroughfare, Hartford Road. (I thought I'd use compass points since us guys SO love directions!)

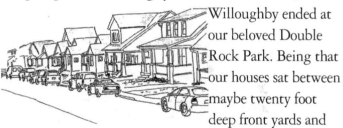 Willoughby ended at our beloved Double Rock Park. Being that our houses sat between maybe twenty foot deep front yards and sixty foot deep back yards, double those yards and you had the width of my block, its back street being Hiss Avenue. Every other street for twenty streets or more ran perfectly parallel to ours, bridged by alleys spotted every quarter mile. Between Hartford and the alley, my block was 1,320 feet long, and our house was equal distance from both corners.

Once, I decided to run away from home. I was seven years old. I found a suitcase in which I stuffed my favorite toys. To my mother's utter, and to me, confusing amusement, I walked out the front door and down the steps to the sidewalk. I wasn't allowed to cross the street so I turned left and walked east to the alley, then north up to Hiss, then left (west) on Hiss to Hartford, south on Hartford to Willoughby, then east again on Willoughby. There I was, back home to a smiling and all-knowing mother!

Although each house was different, to the lost visitor, the streets looked exactly the same, except in our case. The block on which we lived was more than half consumed by my elementary school and its adjoining and gigantic asphalt play-  ground. The old school was a typical dark brick three story rectangular box with windows outlined in thick white concrete. It fronted Hartford Road between Hiss and our street, and the school's backyard was the playground, it too sandwiched between Willoughby and Hiss. It ended at the side of the Heubeck's yard and then jutted past the back of their and our back fences, stopping again on the Hiss side at Widow Smith's side yard. The remainder of the block was houses, north and south, back to back until the alley.

The playground was a source of endless enjoyment. I remember being outside during recess, waving to Mom as she was hanging clothes on the line, or her handing me the occasional forgotten lunch or home work assignment over the fence. When we weren't hanging on the monkey bars, sliding after wax papering the slide, or trying to get the push carousel to fly (on which I became deathly ill, curing for all times motion sickness!), we'd play a host of games: dodge or kick ball, tether ball, hop scotch, or tag, three flys out or touch football. It was our own two acres of asphalt lined off with baseball diamonds and two chainlink backstops in opposing corners. All outdoor activities seemed to either start or finish on the playground, and on many a night, in the pitch dark, we'd be out there riding our bikes. And whenever I was done, I could simply hop the fence into my own backyard.

Of course, being that close had its colossal drawbacks. Mom or Dad were never but an instant from a teacher's conference or witnessing the dreaded beating of erasers on that same playground after school, a sure sign that one of us had been punished. We couldn't use "school" as an excuse for anything nor could we fool the school for a minute. There was simply *no* place to hide!

On my side of the street, in order, were the school, the playground, then the Heubecks, us, the Zitnicks, the Fitzells, the Rueters, and finally the Poteets. Across the street lived the Riechters (until the Gochenours replaced them), Mrs. Schmidt, the Dorseys, and the Glovers; behind us, Mrs. Smith, the Ensors, and the Messicks. Several houses of unknown occupants finished out their side of Hiss Avenue. Remember

these names for there WILL be a test later. Like a
bird watcher, I could distinguish the houses by the
cars that belonged to them. You had to stay awake,
though; there was constant change afoot. But if you
were good, you could even spot the one-upsmanship:
the Huebecks bought the '57 Plymouth Belvedere,
the Fitzells bought a 1959 Buick Lasabre, the Ruters
bought a matching year Pontiac Booneville, the
Glovers had to have the Galaxy Skyliner with the
retractable roof; and so on. Decent, higher end cars
were popping up all up and down the street. The
Poteets outclassed us all, and one could say they were
the envy and genesis for the competition.

My childhood was one of loving and being loved,
playing hard and learning hard lessons. No cell
phones, no X-Box, no distractions except baseball,
music, the occasional cute girl and cars. There were
no contact lenses to lose, bank card numbers to steal,
or Bic pens to use. We'd spend our allowances on
twenty-five cent movies, hula hoops, pee shooters and
candy. Our clothes dried on the line, gay meant you
were happy and grass was something you mowed.
Year after year, I'd ride my bike through the streets,
maturing by the day, noticing every change, no matter how subtle. But, above all, I made darn sure I
knew what was residing in the driveways!

Chapter Three
THE TWO CAR FAMILY

My childhood coincided with a white hot cultural/ industrial revolution. Detroit was tooling up for its most garish two and a half decades, the '50s, '60s and early '70s. Ignited by pent up post depression, post war demand for cars, massive highway projects, and the need for a second car, the Big Three started pumping out literally tons of chrome and fins. In 1945, Americans bought 70,000 cars. In 1950, they bought 6,665,000! By 1955, automobiles sales were $65 billion and had become 20% of Gross National Product. Add a legendary car designer, Harley Earl, a glimpse of James Dean's Porsche Spyder, and a black and white Sylvania featuring Diana Shore inviting us to see the U.S.A. in a Chevrolet, and I was swept hard down current! Staying with the water analogy, for us Boomers, particularly us early Boomers, we found ourselves "drowning" in a sea of cool cars.

So, my generation witnessed the birth of the average man becoming a two car family. As a result, all of us with one car garages (often not used for the car) were forced to put one in the driveway and one in front of the house. And if you used the garage, you still put the other one on the street to avoid the daily, "Can you move the car so I can get mine out?" nag. In my neighborhood, as in most, the streets were especially narrow, and parked cars left a corridor about a car and half wide through which to travel. That interesting tidbit had a large impact on my car memories, and led to an early lesson in driving!

For instance, I remember when Mom went to work for the first time as a salesperson in a children's clothing store. It was a great gig for her and vastly improved our wardrobe. After just several weeks and some complicated gymnastics getting her to and from work, it was determined that she would need her own car. And THAT would officially make us a two car family. After briefly (I mean, very briefly) shopping, Dad brought home a 1958 black Renault Dauphine, the little French car with the "town and country" horn. This model had creamy white interior and our very first, hand crank sun roof. With the exception of Mom, the rest of us

were ecstatic! It was so compact and so, well, European!

She thought it was too small and probably terribly unsafe. In fact, it was *very* small and grossly unsafe (obviously pre-NTSB). Being used, Dad wasn't sure of its lineage (bought it real cheap from a "friend!") and quickly discovered he should have asked more questions. As my brother recalls, the shifter was so sloppy you could barely find a gear, and the poor little thing would overheat after running fifteen minutes. Not finding a leak and confounding Dad, he resorted to carrying a gallon jug of water in the car to replenish the vanishing reservoir. We weren't too smart about the apparent cracked block! But the clincher came one day during Mom's evening commute home. The brakes failed and she spun the thing. A policeman had to comfort her. We kids remember a spirited discussion between her and Dad, and the little Renault had to find a new home.

It was all so short lived! Dad determined to buy American the next time and nothing was more American than a Nash Rambler, which I believe Mom drove with success and fewer complaints for several years. It, of course, sat on the street, too.

Chapter Four
NEARLY KILLED...TWICE!

My first car memory, though, was in Dad's new maroon 1950 Ford, straight six, with a three speed. How could I ever forget? Okay, I was too young to know about car names, transmissions and six cylinder engines, but as someone just shy of six years old, I *do* remember trying to drive that baby while it was parked in front of the house.

Here's the story...the houses which lined Willoughby were a combination of brick and shingle, or all brick or all shingle. Each was different, but most had some sort of front porches and small front yards, which could be manicured with a few short push mower passes (I mean real push... no engine!) Our house was brick on the first floor with a slightly smaller white shingled second story. It was quite unremarkable... a

symmetrical box with two windows on either side of
the front door, itself enclosed in a roofed brick porch.
The front door and porch were six feet off the front
yard on its west side and eleven feet off the concrete
driveway on the east (it was quite the wall to scale!).
Its stout brick steps led down to a ten foot long concrete walk, which itself ended in four more steps to
the sidewalk. Although mostly level, the final four
feet of our front yard dove sharply to the sidewalk,
making that hill just a wonderful lawn mowing experience. Stepping out onto the porch, you could look
over the left (east) brick wall into a cavernous concrete driveway, great for launching balsa wood F-86
gliders or warding off charging enemy soldiers, as it
was the very best machine gun nest in the neighborhood. The streets were neatly lined in sidewalks and
each family, if they had been too lazy to pull into the
driveway or had the afore mentioned second car, simply left it parked in front of the house. That's where
ours was on that fateful day.

The Maroon Ford was a stubby box of a vehicle,
with all the edges rounded over, and a gigantic flat
steering wheel. While playing "driver" one day, I
must have become over zealous; turning the wheel,
grabbing knobs and
shifting levers, and
suddenly sensed
the car moving...
backwards. "Uh
Oh! Now I've done

it! I'm gonna die! And if I don't die, I'm gonna get killed!" I started pulling and shoving everything in arms reach. Behold, my oversized toy rolled to a stop! Whew!! No harm done!

The only slight problem…ever so slight…was that we were now parked (or at least not moving) squarely in front of the neighbor's house, the Zitnicks! Umm…? I eased out of the car, ran up the sidewalk, climbed the steps to the porch, and looked back over the machine gun wall at its new location. It didn't look too bad to me…just down the street a little! I mean, I could still see it….kind of…behind that bush. I slipped into the front door believing no one saw the criminal act or would notice anything askew.

Minutes or hours passed, I'm not sure, but I can remember starting to relax, maybe even forgetting. Then, while playing in the basement, I heard my father's voice coming through the ceiling (it might as well have been God pronouncing judgment)… "What's the car doing in front of the Zitnicks?" And, Mom's startled reply, "What? Where?" "How did…" Then, deadly silence. Do you remember the childhood feeling when your ears grew hot, your stomach turned, and you couldn't feel your legs? That's exactly what happened when I heard Dad say, "Where's Rodger?" It is amazing how young one develops flight instincts! And as guilt hides from justice, it also knows when it's coming! Let me just say here that this event led to the mother of all childhood spankings, you know, the kind where your father emphasizes every word between swats? "YOU, (swat) WILL, (swat) NEVER , (swat)...." A friend recently remarked, "It's a wonder you weren't permanently traumatized, and that cars didn't represent the devil himself!" Actually, it may have had the opposite affect!

I had escaped being killed by my father but I needed even more luck to evade my neighbor. The folks directly to our right were the Huebecks, a very nice German family (our neighborhood was largely Italian, Polish, and German...hummm... wonder how that happened?) They had two children, Bobby and Carol. Bob was my brother's age and Carol older and, to me, the most beautiful woman I'd ever seen. Anyway, Mr. Huebeck drove this huge red and white '57 Plymouth Belvedere (with the Torque-Flite push-button transmission).
The fins on that dude were wicked. We could hear Mr. Heubeck start that Plymouth from anywhere in 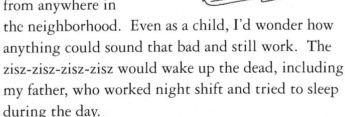 the neighborhood. Even as a child, I'd wonder how anything could sound that bad and still work. The zisz-zisz-zisz-zisz would wake up the dead, including my father, who worked night shift and tried to sleep during the day.

The Huebeck's home was an all-white shingle Tudor, with green shutters, and a side porch on their west side (a great place for army ambushes!), and, on the east, a driveway which separated our house from theirs. It ran from a detached single garage out back, past their house, out to the street. Our back yards were fenced, and I'd climb theirs rather than ours to get into the schoolyard since their rustic mountain stone grille had natural steps built in its side (1, 2, 3 and over), versus our fence which offered no such natural easement. Anyway, their front yard matched ours as well, and the last fifteen feet, although more gently graded, connected at a 20 degree angle with Willoughby.

Every morning, Mr. Heubeck sped backwards out of his drive (the more speed the better) and the rear bumper of his Belvedere would crash and drag on poor Willoughby's increasingly gouged and scared asphalt. It was a sickening sound and the constant talk of the neighbors. Apparently, it didn't bother the Heubecks, as day after day, in and out, he'd crash, punch it into "drive" and head up the street! How could a car live through that?

So, one day I was cruising down the sidewalk on my brother's 26" red metal flake English bike (equipped with the trademark thumb gear shifter, skinny seat, mini saddle bag, and tire pump). My feet barely reached the pedals and staying on the sidewalk was my mother's mandate, for my own safety. Since I was not all together steady on the thing, I could fall over in someone's yard or into their front fence and not be killed by a car in the street. Oh yeah?

I was merrily biking along, tip toes barely touching on each down stroke, gaining on my house when, you guessed it, Mr. Heubeck came roaring backwards down his drive. The timing could not have been more perfect... aaaannnnd CRUNCH!! He hit me square on the upstroke of the pedal closest to the trunk, barely missing my foot and leg, as the car's rear bumper was only inches from its final descent. It simultaneously drove me through the air and swallowed Doug's prize English bike, smashing it under four thousand pounds of chrome and fins! Apparently, the new ring tone of crushing tubular metal rang out with a different enough note that three neighbors, including Mom, ran out of their houses. Mr. Heubeck leaped from the car and ran around back to find me sitting in the middle of the street, dazed, while sprouts of bike parts, carnage like you've never seen, were sticking out from under his bumper. I recall Mom bursting into tears, running into the street after me, a sight in itself which so badly frightened me, I jumped up exclaiming, "I'm okay, I'm okay, I'm REALLY okay!!!" I actually WAS okay with the exception of a few bruises. But within seconds, I had this huddle of aproned mothers surrounding me with poor Mr. Heubeck in the background profusely apologizing to everyone and no one at the same time. Interestingly, that Plymouth hardly ever scraped the ground again. We all kind of knew why!

Chapter Five
THE MG DID IT!

After the '50 Ford, but before the '57 Plymouth,
I had my "first kiss" with a car! Living across the
street diagonally to our right was Doc Reichter, a
local pharmacist, in a little brick home that contained
an undiscovered pleasure. The Reichter house was a
narrow shotgun style, with its garage in the basement
around the back of the house. In fact, the hill that
ended at the Heubecks driveway, leveled to accommodate Willoughby, and then continued its slope down
the Reichter's driveway. Many of the original neighborhood drives were designed as two strips of concrete
evenly divided by a strip of grass, and most everyone
had converted to all concrete or asphalt by the time
I was ten. But the Reichters hadn't and that strip
would serve as the 60' 6" path from pitcher to catcher
many summer days. One honorable mention... the
Heubecks had a cherry tree in their front lawn. The
Reichter house included an all brick porch with half
height brick walls serving as the only fortified

defensive position during massive cherry throwing battles. Boy, did they sting!

Have I wandered again? Forgive me...Mom and I were over visiting, borrowing a cup of sugar or doing the fifties neighbor "drop in" thing, and I remember Doc asking me if I'd like to take a ride in his "sports car!" "What's a sports car?" I thought. But it sounded exciting as no one had ever invited me to do anything remotely like this. With a smile and a "go on" from my Mom, I followed Doc through the kitchen, down narrow basement stairs and into a dimly lit garage where sunlight mingled with dust was peeking through old garage door curtains. The combined smell of gasoline and oil was so pungent that to this very day, gas fumes in a garage are like a time machine back to this one simple episode. There sat a bright red MG TD with camel colored interior and the top down. I had never seen it out in the neighborhood and didn't even know it existed! Doc ushered me past its chrome grille and bullet headlights. Turning me, we squeezed along the tight wall to the passenger door where he lifted me over into the seat. He walked around behind the car, swung open two sagging wooden doors, and then climbed in next to me. He pulled a starter button on the dash, and, of course, I didn't know it at the time, but a little 56 h.p. engine with twin SU carbes sprang to life (capable of 0-60 in 18.2 seconds...gee, wow!).

Being so small, I remember staring at nothing but a wooden dashboard cluttered with chrome-ringed instruments and ivory gauge faces. My only other two views were of Doc, and out through the v-cut door. I had a building thrill of the unknown as he backed out into the sunlight (my first convertible), and then headed up the narrow driveway hill and out onto our street. "Hey, there is my house from a whole new view point!" We gathered speed and the wind was swirling around me while the leafy tree branches passed overhead. What a fantastic sensation, speeding along in the open air, riding in a machine built almost purely for fun! I recall bouncing along through the upshifts, smelling leather and gasoline, and falling utterly in love. I don't remember how long we were out or where we even went, but I'll never forget (and neither does she) bugging my Mom to take me back to Doc's house for "Just one more ride, please?" It seemed that he and his family moved shortly afterwards (probably because they had a 6 year old stalker). And although it wouldn't be the last MG to grace our street, I was forever smitten from a kiss by this little red sports car!

Chapter Six
A BOX OF PAPER HEROIN

Our home had lots going on besides the constant car chatter. My sister was a ballerina, my brother was a Boy Scout, and I was taking accordion and guitar lessons. We boys played little league baseball. When Dad wasn't working (or sleeping) he was writing his first book, "The Breeding of Giant Food Frogs." (No, I'm not kidding. Check the Library of Congress). And, as a skilled amateur artist, he had paintings in various stages, scattered around the house. Dad was also quite a good weekend photographer (the man had an original Hasselblad!) and took pictures of literally everything and anything. "Roddy, look this way... SNAP!"

During his book writing days, he collected jars of frogs in formaldehyde, and shelves lining the basement walls were dense with jars of bloated, dead frogs! I'm not joking! Because the basement housed his dark room (replete with chemical smells), as well as the frogs and the furnace, and occasionally gave way to significant floods, the basement was genuinely creepy. But we willed ourselves to play down there as it was where Dad would build our annual Christmas train garden, and where many of our hide and seek games would conclude. When very young and while riding my tricycle in circles, I struck a gas line to the furnace for which I was forewarned: "Never, ever touch this! Do you hear me?" Yes, another memorable spanking…. "YOU," swat," WILL," swat…

When our parents would go out, leaving Doug as the "babysitter," he and I would conspire and lock my sister in the basement just long enough to have her think she would never get out. I was too young to actually be that devious, but Doug wasn't. Moreover, often just after the parents left, Doug did this *thing* where he would fall down and play dead for a solid hour, not moving a solitary muscle. I'd be crying hysterically by the end and Cheryl, although confident it was a scam, would even start to worry. Are you getting this picture?

My brother and I shared an upstairs bedroom. It wasn't easy for my 16-year-old bro to have his 10 year old kid brother in his room, but the house wasn't that big and there we were, the original odd couple. Cheryl, the queen, had her own room, and therefore deserved whatever teasing we dished out. We wouldn't have had either room had Dad not built the second story on the house, fashioning two bedrooms for his kiddies. Actually, the second story was already there. Dad finished it out…almost. Our room had knotty pine floors, some sort of matching paneling (my first encounter with paneling…), and one foot square white ceiling tiles overhead. We had curtained closets as Dad never got around to making real doors. Our beds were built into each corner of the room because Dad had this nautical acumen (boats are another entire book), and decided to make bunks that looked like cabin beds from a ship. It kind of worked and kind of didn't.

The bedroom never had enough insulation and we'd freeze in the winter and sweat like hogs in the summer, but I loved it. I remember trying to go to sleep in hot summer nights, lying there with the windows open and a fan leaning on the window screen. We were under Dad's strict orders to leave the motor reversed, supposedly sucking the hot air out. I think it took until four each morning before any cool air would creep back into the opposite window. But we'd lie there with barely any clothes on waiting for a whiff of cool. Then I'd pull up the sheet and drift off to sleep. In the winter, we had this grossly dangerous electric heater, resembling a ray gun affixed to a satellite dish. There was also Dad's menacing caution about getting near that thing. After my basement spanking, I retained the lesson. So we kept our distance and consequently froze our hind parts off!

It happened one day that I came home from school to find an old dishwasher box between those beds. "What's with this?" I said, as I approached and peered over its edge. "Holy Cow!" I was staring down at

250 old *Hotrod* and *Custom Car* magazines. "Where did these come from?" I said to no one in particular. I headed downstairs and asked Mom where that treasure trove of mags came from? "Oh, your brother got them from Tommy Poteet. They were throwing them out!" To say that there were 250 magazines was no exaggeration.

So, it all started innocently enough...Doug would take one, I'd take another and around bedtime (mine much earlier than his, but that never kept me from waiting up) we'd mostly look at the pictures and talk about V8s, custom cars and Corvettes; tossing magazines back and forth between our beds and saying, "Hey, look at this one..." This went on for several years with no shortage of fresh images. We learned customizing themes, neat wheel and tire combos, engine tips, and began to develop discriminating tastes as to what was and what was not considered "cool!" And then there were all of the collateral gimmicks to affirm my beliefs...I mean what kid didn't build the Invisible V8 or huge T-Bucket model? And who didn't think that three deuces on a Red engine block or flames on a black Ford weren't the end all!

Listen, I even remember the first time I saw Charlie Hill's 283 Hillborn injected Filthy '40 Willys gasser. Do you remember the album "Big Sound of the Drags"? Santa brought Cheryl a grey portable "stereo" phonograph, a suitcase looking thing whose side speakers were on hinges and optionally detached. They had enough wire to create a twenty foot separation between the speakers. (Or you could feed the wire back into a hole. Remember those?) Since the record player was hopelessly wed to her 45s, we could occasionally commandeer it, switch over to 33.3 and play "Big Sound of the Drags" (along with Peter Paul and Mary and the Kingston Trio). They were perfecting stereophonic sound and the dragsters would

seemingly run from one end of the bed room to the other. This was OUR 3-D! We wore out that album listening to Charlie's runs in the quarter mile and then, behold, I actually saw him live at Capital Drag Raceway!

As you can see, my senses bore a full on frontal assault from an early age. But I found that learning about cars was similar to exercise, it gave me an edge when it came to needing to know...and you needed to know a lot about cars if you lived on Willoughby Road! Take the Poteets, for example...

Chapter Seven
THE POTEETS

You know when you have an "Aha!" moment? It occurred to me sometime along this journey that the Poteet family had an amazing influence in shaping my life. It was both subliminal and very direct. If the MG ignited my car love affair, the Poteet's legitimized it. In fact, they seemed to make everything fashionable and generated an energy that kept the entire neighborhood alive. Theirs was the last house on the left, just before the alley and four houses to our right (east, facing the street). Mom says it was always the most well-kept home and most tastefully decorated. When I'd ride by on my bike, I'd wave to Mrs. Poteet (Mil), check out the cool cars in the driveway or garage and wish I could spend more time with them.

Why? Let's count the ways: 1) they were a big family of boys - Dick, David, and Tommy - and all were great guys, particularly to me; 2) their house was impeccably furnished. (Mom felt the upward calling

towards Ethan Allen Early American furniture because
it "looks so good in the Poteet house"); 3) they had
the only two-car garage in the neighborhood; 4)
Mr. Poteet (Shef) worked at GM for thirty-five years
and had some amazing new cars filling that space; 5)
they had the first RCA color TV in the neighborhood
from which we watched, in living color, "Bonanza"
and "The Wonderful World of Disney." (Dad bought
our first color TV, albeit six years later, because we
hounded him unmercifully after the Poteet experience); 6) they were terrific and versatile musicians,
every last one of them, and they played together as a
family, often for the neighbors. Although they could
switch it up, Mrs. Poteet mostly played piano;
Mr. Poteet, the Guitar; Dick, the trumpet; David, the
drums; and Tommy, the sax. They were the original
Osmonds! And, I became both a drummer and semi-
professional guitarist thanks to David and the Poteets.
Modeling after them, my own two boys (both musicians) and I "jammed" in our basement many times!

If that weren't enough, then there was one of the
best reasons for me: David had the hotrods...did he
ever! Our first remembrance was his "Little Stinker,"
a 1955 Maroon Chevy Bel Air with a white convertible top and custom white roll and pleated interior.
It was decked and shaved with louvers on the hood.
Each lower front quarter panel sported a professionally painted and ever
so cute skunk and the
script "Little Stinker"

over each. When we thought he couldn't outdo himself, David bought a fully customized 1958 Impala, "Turbo Thrust" 348, tri-power (the truck engine!). It had this outrageous candy apple red paint job (I'd never seen glitter in paint!), lowered, decked, shaved, legpipes, again, white roll and pleated interior and the first "four" speed transmission (Borg Warner T-10) I'd ever seen. Remember, this was in 1959, so this car was essen-

tially new and then customized. Four speeds didn't show up until '59, so that was a conversion, all of it extravagantly expensive. And it was Mr. Poteet who drove one of the prettiest production cars of all time, a white 1957 Chevy Bel Air hardtop, with red interior 283, and it was most likely a fuelie, knowing their inclination for "top of the line" everything!

But their colorfulness was forged from sadness. It was a little known fact that the Poteets had a first son who died from Polio, a disease which would find its cure in this same decade. They once had a built-in swimming pool and related his contraction of the disease to the pool. Proven or not, the two car garage now sat where the pool once was. After I was made aware of this, I felt conflicted about loving that garage scene, but wishing it wasn't there. They were quite the family and remained the reigning neighborhood trend setters and car war champions. None of us even considered competing with them.

Chapter Eight
A SCREAMIN' CHEVY!

Yes, I was getting hooked. And while the visual images were working their allure, the actual road experiences were what would alter my DNA. Here's one of the earliest I recall…

My buddy, Jimmy, and I were at the corner malt shop, "Classes," one evening. I remember it was getting pretty dark. I was eleven and yet was given free reign to visit the malt shop as it was literally on the north corner of Hartford and Hiss, directly across from the school and my block. I had the privilege of "guarding" that busy corner as a Safety in the fifth and sixth grades. The family who owned Classes (The Classes) were considered neighbors as
their house extended
out of the back of the
store, and so we were
granted special visit-
ing privileges and

spent a good deal of time there! "Hey, Mr. Class!"
was probably said and heard maybe a thousand times
in my life?

It was a traditional malt shop, positioned on the
corner so that even the front glass door was hung
diagonally on the corner of the building, flanked by
big picture windows, one facing west and one facing
south. Both windows were adorned with Gold gilded
lettering; "Classes Malt and Candy Shop!" Inside you
were greeted on the left with a plastic domed popcorn machine, its yellow light and its built-in bag
dispenser inviting a five-cent purchase of hot (okay,
warm) popcorn. It was an early version of automated
vending! Behind it, the back wall was lined with a
six foot long glass case of penny and nickel candy,
which itself gave way to a twenty foot long wooden
counter replete with permanent chrome stools topped
in red vinyl. There were two wooden booths on the
opposite wall scarred with the obligatory pen knife
carvings of who was in love with whom! I maintained a steady and loyal love affair with the cutest
blond, Janet Sealy, from the first to the fifth grade,
and I am certain our names were carved in the left
booth. And you never left Classes without a box of
Good and Plenty, Juicy Fruits, or Sugar Daddys!

Jim and I were standing at the far end of the
counter. I remember Doug busting through the
front door (he was seventeen), walking past Jimmy,
grabbing me by the arm, doing an about face and
marching us back towards the exit. I searched his

expression for a sign. Did I detect a slight grin?
"What did I do? What about Jimmy?" I pleaded as
he was yanking me along. "Good bye, Jimmy!" he
said over his shoulder, and, once on the sidewalk, he
shoved me through the open window and into the
back seat of a primer colored '55 Chevy, two-door
post with the passenger door roped closed. "What's
going on?" I demanded. "Shut up! We're going for
a ride!" Doug said.

John Bupp,
Doug's high school
buddy, was driv-
ing, some other kid
was in the front seat,
and Doug and I were
riding in the back. Bupp cranked over the engine
and right away I knew the body was a hoax. The
rat trap sounded glorious! "Is this a real hotrod?" I
asked my brother. "Just enjoy it!" he said. I noted it
had a "floor shifter" with a white cue ball knob (self
installed shifters were the mark of serious rodders),
and although there was enormous play in the shifter,
Bupp seemed to locate the mysterious first gear. We
edged away from Classes, turning right up Hartford
road and out, away from town. Doug whispered in
my ear, "John just put a bored and stroked 283 Vette
engine in this thing. We're on the test run! You
better hang on little brother!" To tell me an engine
was "bored and stroked" was code for "this ain't your
papa's V8!" ...a bedtime magazine lesson. Second,

when my brother recited the "hang on" speech, his face took on a maniacal look that said, "If I have ever joked with you, I'm not joking now!" I've seen that look many times since. He was and remains clearly sicker than me.

Fifteen minutes later we were lined up in the middle of a country straightaway, with my brother and his pals counting backwards from five. I was petrified, thinking if Dad knew I was in this car, he'd kill my brother, then me...and then Jimmy, who wasn't even with us! John was revving the engine (no tach, of course) higher on each successive number. The road was deserted and the one strong left head-light (the right one, I later saw, was dangling from its wires, facing the road!) cast a beam on a two-lane asphalt road with just a glimpse of green pasture on either side. Then John sidestepped the clutch. Bang! The small block screamed to life, the four barrel broke open in a sound like I had never heard. The back end broke loose, first left and then right, and the '55 caught traction just in time for Bupp to slam the overmatched three speed into second gear. Lean-ing into the wheel, he wound out the engine to an ungodly howl, wind whipping through the open win-dows, and with an exaggerated elbow whip, pulled it hard back into third, gathering speed for what seemed like forever. Then he lifted off the accelerator, letting the over achieving Vette engine catch its breath. We slowed; he revved, downshifted to second, and braked to some non-blurring speed.

The boys started screaming and slapping everything in the car, using words I was not allowed to hear, let alone say! I sat visibly shaken, but never feeling more alive! This was a naughty pleasure as I was reminded more than once by Doug, "Don't tell Mom and Dad, or I'll kill you!" John found a farmhouse driveway to slip into and back out of, and I could tell by the adrenaline, once wasn't enough for these boys. Heading in the opposite direction, they stopped dead center in the road and played the same counting game. This time, Bupp let it loose with even more pedal and aggression. The left front end torqued in the air, surely redlining first, banging it into second, and removing what little rubber was left on the tires! I found myself getting into the second run; screaming with the guys and becoming the cool (fool) little brother. Can you imagine now just how unstable and crude that thing was in 1955? Do you understand how fortunate I am to be alive? Just wait…it gets worse. And there IS a God!

John treated me to another ride sometime later, this in a borrowed white over blue '55 Bel Air. The car was equipped with the 265 V8, four barrel, and its owner had transplanted the column three speed to the floor, using a shifter from a company named "Hurst." It was my introduction to Hurst shifters. The whole experience was much more civilized; just John, my brother and me, leaving from the house in broad daylight like normal humans. We drove away, me sitting in the middle edge of the backseat, leaning on the front seat between my brother and his pal. Threading between the parked cars down Willoughby, we were headed to the junior high school. John turned onto this part of Hiss Avenue, a decent, wide straight away running right next to the school. (No, it wasn't in session!!)

He brought the car to a stop in the middle of the street, the sign that we were about to make a drag run, revved three or four times with increasing fervor, dumped the clutch and launched. Again, the little Chevy bit down with alternating wheel spin and traction, sweet V8 taching up, all going as planned until John slammed it into second. Being young and naïve, I had never heard a transmission blow, nor knew it was possible. The sound was akin to an ape vigorously shaking a metal box full of nuts and bolts, plus a few washers for added affect. In disgust, Bupp said the word I wasn't allowed to repeat, and my brother said it a split second after John's utterance. So now we only had first and third and the boys had to nurse the borrowed Chevy back to the house. It was quite the learning curve for me, and etched in my mind how wonderfully expensive this fun can be!

Chapter Nine
THE CORVETTES

Our house was ten blocks north of the shopping district, Parkville. To walk there meant giving up a couple of hours. But also, the privilege of walking implied being old enough to do so. That honor was fully bestowed on me when I was around ten years old and until then, was awarded progressively. Depending on my age, and never without filing a flight plan, I'd wander further and further from the house on Saturdays. I learned to expect the obligatory, "… but be careful!" Those words were my permission slips and as long as I didn't abuse the privilege, I was permitted to travel further with each successive trip. When it came time to walk all the way to Parkville, I knew I had arrived! When I could walk past Parkville to Hamilton, an additional mile south, one way, I felt all grown up and trusted. Mom was terrific, and the towns were safe. It was life in the fifties!

Parkville city center was Mecca, home to the City Wide Hobby Shop, from which most of my AMT car models originated (plus a fleet of very cool model airplanes, tanks, ships, and gobs of Testors glue!). Parkville was also home to the Colony Theater, the Parkville Bowling Alley (duck pins, of course), Shultie and Trity Five and Ten Cent Store, the A & P, and the second most loved store after the Hobby Shop, Sunny Surplus! I mean what kid didn't have a fake M1 rifle, a canteen, a machete, and sergeant stripes sown on their jacket?

And like so many of us in the fifties, for 25 cents we'd spend all day Saturday in the Colony, entering in daylight, leaving in the dark; arriving in the sunshine, leaving in the rain (or occasional snow), eating boxes of JuJu Beads, Dots, or Good and Plentys, and poking your buddy to watch all of the best parts of

 the movie the second time through. Mom once embarrassingly showed up in the middle of a movie and drug me out by the arm after learning that Cheryl and Doug had taken me to see "The Creature from the Black Lagoon!" But, walking to and from Parkville was always an adventure as we'd climb on brick walls, meander in and out of store fronts, play army behind walls and trees, linger at the Colony to see what movies were coming, and try not to step on a crack and break our poor mother's backs.

Okay, I'm getting to the Vettes, but I must make more stop… Another neighbor, the Dorseys, (across the street, a little to our left) owned a dive shop called "Divers Den." Yes, I mean a scuba diving shop, in Parkville… in the fifties! And it's still there, on Hartford road, claiming to be the oldest dive shop in Maryland. I believe it! The eldest son held some sort of world duration record submerged in a glass tank on TV. We all watched while he became a local folk hero and was at least regionally famous, as was their store. Of course, we never failed to walk through their shop half way to town, say our hellos, gawk and wonder over outer-space looking tanks, hoses and rubber masks. Then, we'd head on our way. I, nor any of my family, can recall the cars they drove. That's highly unusual for me. I guess the aura of scuba diving must have overshadowed everything!

My second love affair with an automobile came on one such Parkville jaunt when I was twelve years old. Jimmy and I were walking past the Sunoco station, just a few blocks from home and there sat a Midnight Blue 1963 split window coupe Corvette, idling outside of the garage bay. Corvettes had already

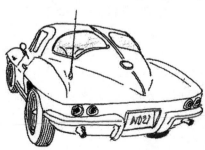

become meaningful to me and would stake out a prominent place in my car history, beginning with Doug's buddy, Rick Howard, and his fabulous four speed, '62, red 327/300 horse convertible. But here parked before me was an automotive creation that would become one of the rarest and sought after collector cars on earth. I had learned that Corvette was about to introduce its next generation of cars, something called the C2 body style. But on the street, it would be known simply as the "Stingray"! It would be based on the Larry Schinoda's Macho Shark I concept car which every car loving boy had seen in pictures.

Jimmy and I were in mid-step when either he or I first saw it, and we did that thing where you look at one another astonished, eye brows raised, eyes wide, mouths forming "Os," speechless. We crossed the station parking lot and moved in on it carefully, respectfully, its 300 SL-ish roof cut driver's door standing open. I was stunned by its beauty and symmetry; tail pipes protruding from the rear facia, knock-off wheels, hidden headlights swiveled shut as if to not interrupt the graceful body lines. Its bulging musclar fenders and low stance elevated it in my mind to Ferrari status. And what a fantastic instrument cluster! A huge and all business tach and speedometer which read an unbelievable 160 m.p.h., (and we had no doubts it could achieve every bit of that and more!) lurked behind a fabulous three spoke wheel. And the rear window was outrageous, split in two, giving it an amphibious quality deserving of its nickname.

The owner, who was also the Sunoco station owner, walked out of the office towards the car, sensed we kids were getting our first drink, and let us linger a minute longer. We asked some questions, but I don't remember any of the answers except him saying, unsolicited, "It's a Z06!" I had no idea what a Z06 was until he told us that just 199 were being made for racing. I later learned all had the L84, 327 fuelie pumping 360 horses, an anti-roll bar, 20% larger brakes, beefed shocks, and huge 36.5 gallon gas tank, all for an additional $1,818.45 over a $4,257 sticker.

During the next year, the Sunoco '63 morphed into the race car it was born to be with the addition of competition numbers centered in huge white circles on the doors, hood and roof, and wicked looking flat black sidepipes. Jimmy, my other pals and I talked incessantly about that Vette as if it were a god, choosing lowly Parkville to reside. Thinking back, I was an early eye witness to one the extraordinary sports cars of all time. Other Corvettes would follow, including several for my brother and me. But I was forever changed by one five minute event.

So, what about Rick's 62 Vette? It was the last of its breed and remains one of my favorite cars. Its black leather interior, smart looking rear antenna and aggressive rake enthralled me to the point where I spoke of little else and worked it into every conversation…"My brother's best friend has a Vette!" "Did I tell you that Doug's friend, Rick, has a Corvette?"

"You know, that reminds me, Doug's friend has a Vette!" I don't recall how many times I was told to "Shut up!"

My most colorful memory was when Rick brought my brother home in the wee hours one morning. I usually woke when Doug came home, (and so did my parents for some reason). I idolized Doug and wanted to get in on whatever he was doing. And with that idolization, I'd just bug the living heck out of him! Of course, I began to realize that his late night carousing wasn't without some law breaking, and I took it upon myself to make sure he was staying sober and leaving the women alone. He still won't let me forget that I'd make him walk a straight line in the bedroom at two in the morning. Not too hard to see why he hated sharing a room with little brother, ah? ("Ah" for my Canadian readers...).

Our front bedroom window was huge and extended almost to the floor. I lost count of the times I'd crawl out of bed on summer nights, sit in front of it, lean my head into the screen and listen to all sorts of conversations spoken over the rumble of an idling V8 or a British sports car exhaust. There was Paul Luca's 1959 Ex-state trooper car, 348 cu. in. motor, 3 speed, in which he and my brother terrorized unsuspecting drivers with fake pull-overs and excuses to speed. Or the dove grey Austin Healey bug-eye Sprite that Rick Howard first owned. He yanked the muffler off, painted a Budweiser can grey and installed it on the otherwise straight exhaust in

case he had to show the cops "a muffler!" There was
the Bupp Chevy, or my brother's own 1959 Bright
gold MGA. She was a beauty, with red leather interior, wire wheels and whitewall tires. Having famous
Lucas electrics on board (The Prince of Darkness!),
that *beauty* would run about one out of three days.
Oh, how he'd curse that thing in the mornings when
it wouldn't start, and once even broke his thumb
using the optional engine crank!

The Vette rolled up to the house, and I heard a
door slam. The night air was carrying their voices.
I crawled from bed and assumed my perch. I heard
Doug say, "No, Rick, 'ya gotta leave quietly, man!'"
Doug might as well have gotten in the thing and
screamed up the street
himself, taunting
Rick that way. You
almost knew what was
coming as he tached
up several times, held the next rev momentarily,
dropped the clutch and lit up the rear tires for a good
100 feet (which my buddies and I carefully walked off
the next day, toe to heel...okay so my foot was only
9 inches long!). Let's say he left a lasting impression.
So much so that the house phone rang the instant
Rick was grabbing second gear and some traction.
Through the floors I heard Dad apologizing to
Mrs. Schmidt across the street (she'd call with great
regularity). It didn't sound like a pleasant conversation, and Doug hadn't made it through the front door

before Dad greeted him. I remember shifting from exhilaration at such a raw display of horsepower and authority flaunting, to utter fear at living in my own house.

Had that been the only incident, we might have learned a lesson and laughed it off, but not Doug and not Dad! There were many such clashes when it came to hotheads, hotrods and who was making the rules. The tension between the two had been increasing over such behavior, but this was a grand doozy!! It occurred to me that rebellion was a byproduct of a good hotrod and rodder. I decided to let my brother carry that mantle as I, instead, would enjoy it as an artist: right proportions, sounds, colors, speeds, and thrills.

Chapter Ten
BLACK CARS THAT MATTERED...

As I reflected on this period of my life, there were four other car memories which stuck like liquid nails...all of them for different reasons, and all of them black!

One of my other best friends was Buddy Messick. He lived behind us or, more accurately, behind the Fitzells, and his house fronted Hiss Avenue. I have some fond memories of Bud....when very little; Buddy and I would climb into Spot's doghouse, the Fitzell's mutt, together WITH Spot. It was crowded. We literally wore a path between our houses. Once, while on that path, I gouged my knee on the corner of a cinder-block, gashing it deep enough for my first stitches. Like most everything else, Doctor Goodman was at the end of our block, and just across Hartford road from the school. Mom rushed me there and being the modern doctor he was, he poured raw Methylate into the open wound and started stitching.

The stinging was so outrageous that I never felt the needle and thread!

Bud and I palled around together when Jimmy and I weren't hanging out. Buddy was more my "music" friend, and when I was learning guitar, his parents bought him a yellow Stratocaster and Fender Amp so that he could learn too. We would swap turns at each other's houses, Buddy with his electric and I with a classical guitar (Dad bought from a friend at work), and we'd attempt to play songs together. We ended up going to his house more than mine because Buddy hated dragging that amp between our houses. Our other neighborhood friend, Gary Ensor, was two years older than us, and he wanted to be a drummer, a la Dave Poteet. He rigged up a concoction of boxes and birdcages as his first drum kit. He and it were horrible! We languished in the basement trying to do the band thing, but it went nowhere quickly, and each pealed off to further improve our individual skills.

I smile when I remember that Buddy and Gary were all about rock and roll while I was into folk music (again, thanks to an older brother owning every Kingston Trio, Limelighters and Peter Paul and Mary album made). We had epic arguments over which style was better and consumed several summers with the back and forth. Buddy and I became better guitarists, and Gary a great drummer; all as if to prove each other wrong. As providence unfolded, they eventually formed a band with three other distant neighborhood guys and named themselves "The Grapes of Wrath." They were thirteen at the time. By sixteen, they were cooking. At twelve years old, I convinced my brother to take me to "Patches Fifteen Below," a coffee house named after the owner, Patches, whose shop was fifteen steps down in the basement of a Parkville store. Clever! I played at "Hootenanny Night," which was every Sunday evening, and won a permanent gig as long as I had a ride there. I also played every school and church event I could talk my way into during the next few years. Thinking I was really "the pro," I tried to prove that my music was where it was at, but Buddy and Gary had the last laugh, eventually becoming the best band in Maryland (winning Maryland's battle of the bands in 1965), playing Stones, Animals and Beetles stuff, and went on to make successful record albums. I succumbed and played with them for six months when Buddy broke his arm. It was a bitter sweet role!

One more "Bud" story... his Mom entered Buddy's name in a sweepstakes at the Parkville A&P, and he won a brand new 26" red and white Shwinn bicycle. He excitedly announced to me that he was on his way to Parkville to pick up his bike, and I gathered our friends and waited at my house for his return and promised "fly by!" Sure enough, Buddy made the turn onto Willoughby and was proudly riding this beautiful Shwinn, with whitewall tires and handlebar streamers, down the center of the road. It was a big bike for Buddy, and just as he passed the house, waving to us as if he were on a parade float, he started wobbling, lost control and crashed into the street. We stood in disbelief. Could that have just happened to his new bike (forget Buddy!)? But reason overwhelmed us, and we could see buddy was hurt. I raced inside to get my Mom and we, together, ran to his rescue. The poor boy was covered in road rash, and as Mom led him back to our house, I grabbed his askew handlebars, righted his scratched and tattered new bike, and followed behind. Several years ago, Buddy and I reunited for lunch, laughing hysterically over how much pink Mecruachrome stains covered Buddy's body. He said, "Your Mom got a little crazy on me!" and I said, "At least it wasn't Methylate!"

Black car, black car...yes...umm, Buddy and I had just turned the corner onto Willoughby when he said, "Hey look, there's a hearse in your driveway!" We were still the length of the school and playground away. But I too could see a big black station wagon, with its rear sticking out into Willoughby. "What's a hearse?" I asked, picking up the pace. "That's a station wagon they put dead people in!" Buddy replied. "You mean, when people die, they come and get you in that?" I asked, voice raised and now jogging. "Yep!" Buddy said confidently. "Naw, that's not

 my house." I said. "Yes it is! Somebody died at your house!" Buddy was convinced. In a panic, I

broke into a flat out run, leaving Buddy in my wake (no pun intended).

My first recollection of the "concept" of death came to me while at church. I was very young and sitting between Mom and Dad when I heard the preacher announce, "And we all must die someday..." to whom I openly inquired, apparently of the entire church (and to my parent's forever embarrassment), "Do I have to die too?" Yeah, I was just catching on to the whole "death" thing!

So what was I going to discover when I ran in the house? I knew that I had left only a short time before and everyone was very alive, but what if Mom, Dad or my sister were now "dead"? Or, my brother, maybe Dad actually DID kill 'im! I remember bursting through the front door in tears, screaming "Who died?" To my instant relief, there were my parents sitting comfortably in the living room. I flew into Mom's arms, and, after a Moment, sensed we were accompanied by a stranger. "Honey, this is Mr. Van Horn. He's a friend of your Dad's and served with him in England during the war. No one died. He just dropped in from New Jersey!" Well, it's not everyday that your have a hearse in your driveway. You can imagine what the neighbors thought. So much so, that Mom made Mr. Horn pull the thing in our garage. You can also guess what my next question was..."Is there a dead person in that station wagon?" "Well, as a matter a fact," said Mr. Horn, "yes, there is. I was heading back to Jersey after a 'pick up' and thought I'd stop by to see your Dad!" How unbelievably weird was this? I was half expecting to hear Rod Serling's voice say, "Rodger is about to find out that Mr. Horn, a fine gentlemen from another dimension of time and space, is his ride into the Twilight Zone!"

If that wasn't enough, Dad and Mr. Horn decided to go "out on the town," leaving the aforementioned station wagon, including a dead person, in our house. I recall that we were totally and collectively creeped out! Mom recalls giving them an earful when they finally returned home, very late and neither man anywhere close to sober! By the way, it was a black 1961 Cadillac with grey curtains and fancy chrome scrolls. I didn't care to know any more!

My next life shaping car event happened in late 1961. I was ten. Mom's new job was a hit and had its perks! Her clothing store owner was a Mr. Cohen, a nice Jewish gentleman. He assessed just how bright my mother was and in no time made her the store manager. He really valued her and believed that behind her was a family of trustworthy individuals. His trust of her was so great that on Saturdays he would allow my brother to come pick up, wash, wax, and return his 1960, 356B black Porsche coupe with red leather interior. I'm confident that we weren't anywhere near that trustworthy.

Prior to its first visit to the Piersant house, Doug felt obligated to school me on the attributes of Porsches and what to expect. It was a routine we

often followed when
Doug knew a very
cool car was about
to grace our home.
Doug recited sto-
ries of their amazing

power and handling against cars twice their size. In
the four cylinder world, it had few rivals. He called
it the "bathtub" Porsche and although I couldn't see
the resemblance, it somehow fit. I later learned on
my own that it was the brainchild of Dr. Ferdinand
"Ferry" Porsche, and first produced in 1948. They
had tubular frames, and were lightweight, precisely
engineered; hand built, and were considered the first
production Porsches. The U.S. started importing
them in 1955 through only one man, Max Hoffman,
known for doing all of his importing with a handshake, no written contracts. Porsche made 76,000
356s through 1965. That's when the famed 911
series started. (My brother and I've owned a few of
those…but that's for later chapters). They made
30,963 "B" Porsches, like Mr. Cohen's, from 1959
through 1963. It ran a 1600 CC 4 cylinder with twin
Solex carbs, or one could opt for the Super or Super
90, whose upgrades included a counterweighted
crank, sodium-filled valves and twin Solex P40-II
carburetors.

Doug finished his waxing, and sensing it was
nearing time to fire her up, with no urging, I climbed
in for the trip back to the store…well, not quite

directly back to the store (remember the trustworthy comment?) I was raptured by its good looks and superior quality. I sat in the passenger seat and was encased in rich, bright red leather. Oh, the smell! It seemed to me that all the chrome and gadgets found on huge Cadillacs and Olds were quietly outclassed by this meticulous little machine. It was my first exposure to one of these outstanding German cars and the privilege to ride in one, and the corresponding bragging rights, had my head spinning! I remember sitting a few inches off the ground, and, unlike Rick's Bugeye Sprite, there was an awareness of substantial metal around me. We pulled off and I immediately appreciated its quick handling and low center of gravity. Doug was being ultra careful and a "good driver," knowing very well his neck depended on its safe return. But as he became more comfortable, he'd push the Porsche's limits further and further. And to see just how well it handled, we headed to an area known as Lock Raven reservoir, a manmade lake whose roads followed its snaking shoreline for several miles. After all, there were many routes one could take to get back to Mom's store and this one was, well, was utterly indirect, and clearly not one of them! Hey, we were driving a Porsche!

I recall as the first switchbacks came upon us, Doug geared down, headed hard into the curve, accelerated through and out towards the next bend. Then, he downshifted, braked slightly and accelerated hard into the next one. There are about twenty switchbacks, and he heeled and toed his way through each, the 356 responding to his every command. Remember, these were not seat belt days, so I had to stay planted in my seat with handfuls of dashboard and door handle. But what a rush! The precision four cylinders revved freely and smoothly, and I discovered that a four banger could really deliver the goods. This brief experience set me up for a lifetime of Porsche enjoyment and has led me to believe there has been no car in history that better symbolizes both unparalleled quality and absolute performance.

Chapter Eleven

OKAY, THE OTHER TWO BLACK CARS...

Then there was the black Galaxy! Like a "birder" (that's what you call a birdwatcher...yeah, I didn't know either!), who can tell one Robin from the next, car guys have developed a critical eye for variations and nuances within the brands. If '63 and '64 convertible Vettes were next to one another, we could see immediately that the '64 doesn't have hood grates. One is hard pressed to find other obvious differences. I started my car watching by learning to look for fender badges. Although Ford sported V8 emblems in the early 50's, Chevy didn't join the V8 race until 1955. When that first "V" showed up underneath the '55 Chevy taillights, I learned there was a 265 Cube V8 residing under the hood. And from that point forward I and my pals would check out every hood, trunk, front fender or front quarter panel to tell us the car's secrets. In 1957, a set of flags over the vaunted insignia "Fuel Injection" on the upper fender of a Bel Air, told us that there was a 283 horse, 283 cubic inch engine aboard. From 1956 through 1958, Chevrolet added a gold or chrome "V" on the hood and trunk to indicate they were running either a 283 or 348 cube motor. It was '58 when the Impala was born and the "V" over which flags flew and a deer "leaping" graced the upper rear quarter panel. But the ultimate thrill was spotting a 1962 Chevy whose very front fender noted a V with flags and the numbers 409 underneath. We had all heard rumors in 1961 that an engine had been born with

380 horsepower, but it proved true, affirmed in magazine articles. It immediately gained the status of holy grail when, in 1962, we discovered it devel-

oped 409 horsepower using two Carter AFB four barrels and came with a positraction rear. It was the fastest machine on earth, sung about by the Beach-boys ("She's Real Fine, My 409") and drag raced by the likes of Don Nickleson and Dave Strickler who proved one could turn mid 12's in the quarter mile in a street car. Also in 1962, Chevy added the hallowed "SS" (Super Sport) name to their line up, essentially sealing the deal for having the coolest cars on earth.

If Chevys were the coolest cars, Chrysler was winning the cubic inch war and sneaking up on the automotive world one engine at a time. They were

thinking performance long before the other guys and
in the '50s developed the first generation Hemi's, the
383 and 1961 the Max Wedge 413 "RB" engines,
which produced 375 horsepower. For all of us car
guys, seeing these in magazines under the hood of a
Chrysler C-300 or an Imperial told us that Chrysler
was thinking "racing," but just not getting the press.
Like GM's Cadillac (390 cubic inch), Buick's 410/325
h.p. Pontiac's 389/360 (the real hotrod in 1959!)
and Oldsmobile's 394/315 they appealed to an older,
better healed class. We all knew they were not the
choice of us common folk, particular those of us in a
younger crowd. Interestingly, Chrysler would go on
to have some of the most outrageous car/horsepower
packages in the early '60s, but at the turn of the
decade, they hardly had the money to figure it all out.
It was said that their engineers "backed into" lighter
cars and bigger engines making them an unbeatable
force on the drag strip '64 and beyond.

So, where was Ford? Yeah, they were making
hotrod Lincolns with 352 cubic inch engines and had
the cool 1955 through '57 baby birds with 292 and
or optional 312 displacements. As a matter of interest, my dentist currently has an original "F" bird...
supercharged 312 developing 340 horses, and the
only European bound T-Bird ever made. Its speedo
is in "kilometers!" Top that! Anyway, it was a little
known fact that the Blue Oval motivated Chevy to
bore out their 348 to 409 inches when, in 1960, the
352 "FE" Interceptor Special engine cranked out a

potent 360 horsepower. In response to Chevy's 360 h.p./409 feet of torque, Ford introduced its first big block 390 engines with a three-two barrel set-up in 1961. It was rated 401 horses and 430 foot pounds of torque (interestingly, Ford had no visible out-side emblems on the 1960 Ford so we couldn't tell whether it was running a six or a 390. We had to look for dual exhaust!) And, it was 1961 when Ford put their "bird" badge on the lower front quarter panel with the number 390 notched in its center, a very cool statement! Of course, not to be outdone, Chevy then dialed their '62 base 409 engine to 380 horses and kicked their two-fours engine up to 409 h.p. @ 420 ft/lbs of torque.

So what does this have to do with black cars? As Hiss Avenue was the back border street to our block, Acton Avenue was the back avenue to our neighbors across the street. We would walk pass Acton as the first of many streets on our way into Parkville. But it may have well been on another planet as we seldom ventured down Acton and certainly knew no one who lived over there. It, too, was connected by the same alley as it led from Hiss to Willoughby and Wil-loughby to Acton. One day, while riding my bike down the alley to Acton, I came upon a black '63 Ford Galaxy with red interior and a four speed trans-mission. "What's this?" I said. On it lower panel the Bird introduced me to the 406 cubic inch engine. "Wow...406!" I had to look twice. Where did that come from? In normal fashion, I high-tailed it to my buddy Jim's house, and convinced him to grab his bike and follow me to this momentous discovery! We peddled up to it and started our back and forth banter about its origins as if it had dropped out of

space. Incidentally, it was parked in the alley beside the house where we had dropped an M-80 (when firecrackers were more like dynamite than not) into an open cinderblock wall…not to be soon forgotten! Anyway, we made it our mission to ask enough questions of the older guys in the neighborhood until we had a semblance of truth. No one knew the owner, but it definitely belonged to that house, vaulting whoever the person was into celebrity status.

And so it appeared Ford was on the march! Okay, it wasn't the glamorous 409, but a "big block" was gracing the streets of my neighborhood. We also learned that 405 horses and 448 foot pounds of torque were resting under that hood. Still not the 409, but a solid lick at the leader! It was huge news to all of the Willoughby and Hiss boys, and we had a new champion living in our midst. It was the car that helped me focus on Ford's hotrod future and the coming of the most potent engine of that era, the 427 "Cammer," and the most wicked car of all time and my standard to which all cars would be later judged, the AC Cobra.

There is one other black car honorable mention...
my Aunt Jinny and Uncle Bob lived in the histori-
cal hamlet of Saint Michaels on the eastern shore
of Maryland. It was where my Mom grew up and
we kids spent our summers. St. Michaels was just
a "waterman" town, quiet and lazy, with just a few
hundred residents, all living on a narrow peninsula
dividing the Chesapeake Bay. St. Michaels today
is sought after real estate; a haven for Mercedes and
Rolls, but when I was growing up, it was a poor and
quiet little fishing town. Mom's family, like most
of her neighbors, made its living from crabbing and
clamming and my Uncle Bob on many occasions took
me out in his old wooden fishing scow, centered with
a huge single cylinder engine. It was moored at a
ramshackle dock along with thirty other long white
work boats, with miniature cabins crammed near the
bow. I'd sit on a board of worn and blistered paint
wedged between the gunnels; with crabbing nets, old
work baskets and yards of dirty rope surrounding me.
Getting to your destination was a lesson in military
patience. The Back River had a peacefulness and
beauty one learned to acquire from hundreds of these
slow rides. The occasional sighting of a REAL stingray or shark would be fodder for weeks. Glimpses
of wild life on the shores never ceased to thrill me.
When I wasn't staring at the shoreline, I'd sit, elbows
on knees, starring down at the water "in" the boat (I
swear, we were half sinking at all times), laced with
psychedelic patterns of purple and silver gasoline and

recall always trying to find a fresh dry place to put my feet. The "interior" water would vibrate to the rhythm of that one lung motor, hour after hour, forming perfect circle patterns which radiated in and out, in and out...putt, putt, putt, putt...you just wanted to scream from boredom! We'd finally get down to crabbing, and the sheer terror of Uncle Bob netting a huge blue channeler crab, tossing it in a basket near me, missing, and having the clawed creature chase me around the bottom of the boat, would wake me from the long and arduous wait and remind me of this most rewarding experience and lifestyle.

These were simple folks living in simple times. For as many years as I could remember, Uncle Bob drove a black '49 Ford. It was all they could afford, well into the '60s. And for an equal number of years I never remember it running faster than 25 miles per hour, at the very tops! We had the same speeds, boat or car: slow and slower! I can remember once, when we sped up to 25, Uncle Bob said so humorously and in his country twang, "We're flying now, hun!" I still use that line! These rank as my most priceless memories.

Chapter Twelve
DAD'S TURN!

Dad worked third shift until I was twelve, slept a good portion of the day, and then launched into his many projects, including not quite finishing out the second story on our house. His parents were Italian immigrants who came to Baltimore in the early 1900's, and Dad and his sister were raised to be hard workers and money pinchers. No matter what the neighbors were buying, particularly cars, we were going to be frugal. His motto was "Keep it and keep it cheap!"

Although he passed away in 1994, he was a good and loving man, marvelously talented, a caring father and a wonderful provider. Shortly after his death, Mom asked me to take his tools, and as I was picking through them, I discovered he had a good, better, best of everything. In other words, when he needed a tool, he'd run to Walmart and buy the cheapest one he could find. Then following the progression, I'd find another model that was a better brand, and then still another which I know cost him dearly. I swear, I found ten triplekits of tools. It made me smile. Perhaps this pattern reflected his upward mobility at the newspaper, or just his frustration at always hoping to prove the cheap one WAS good enough to do the job, but as David Crobsy sang, "He never failed to fail!" It is so funny to me that had he bought the best one the first time, he would have saved himself a minor fortune. His cars reflected the same buying pattern.

We were either wearing him down or warming him up, I wasn't sure which. And in 1960, something magical occurred. Surrounded by ever nicer vehicles and my brother's constant influences, which included friends dropping by in their Sprites, MGAs, Austin Healeys, and then the Vettes (oh, the Corvettes!), Dad started to crack. He didn't break easily, but some influence must have finally screwed itself into his brain. The Lou Piersant car chronology for my first ten years went like this...a '49 Buick (used), a 1950 Maroon Ford, straight six, three speed, no radio (new, but stripped), a 150 two door post 1956 Chevy, three speed, no radio (bought new, which we drove as a family of five to Colorado in August ...very comfortable...), the Renault (used, and thoroughly abused), then the Salmon (we didn't call it Pink) and the Grey Nash Rambler, three speed, no radio, (extremely used, but it did have cool reclining seats).

Then Lou bought my brother his first car...a baby blue Henry J Kasier, this time a four cylinder, three speed, and no radio (indescribably used!). Remember the Henry J? It was built by Kaiser-Fraiser Corporation from '50 to '53, and had those Cadillac muted fins and taillights, a Fordish grille, and a four cylinder 68 h.p. engine. In 1953 they added an 80 h.p. six to the line and marketed it through Sears as the "Allstate"! Doug wanted it because, "J's were being made into Dragsters!" In an attempt to make it look dragsterish, he popped off the hubcaps, painted the wheels bright red, and put on 5" portawalls (fake whitewalls). He tells the story that he and his buddy, Rick Howard, were driving it in the rain one day in literal hysterics because the windshield wipers weren't anywhere close to touching the window. But they had to pull over from near black-out laughter when one of the wipers flew completely off and hit the car next to them.

Back to Dad… then there was the base model, turquoise 1960 Ford wagon, straight six, three speed on the column, WITH a radio, but also with an awful bronze colored interior (and, again, used…of course). We were momentarily embarrassed, but being mortified by one of the Piersant rides had become commonplace, and we managed to get over embarrassment quickly. It just seemed like Dad was hopelessly cheap and boring, and everyone knew and accepted it.

Then it happened…we weren't sure; maybe it was a promotion at work, or he might have joined the Mafia. Either way, Dad brought home a beautiful 1958 black and white two tone T-Bird with matching interior. Gorgeous! I mean, drop dead gorgeous!

This "Squarebird" (as they were called) had a honkin' 352 V8, Cruise-A-Matic (what, no three speed?), these radical looking dual headlights; a ground scooping, gaping grill, and a dazzling interior. Needless to say, we were speech-

less! And of course, he quickly burst our bubble by saying, "I'm only test driving it!" "Well, heck, if you're test driving, then you must be thinking about buying one, right Dad?" "Na...just lookin!" he said. Well, it remained a fixture at the house for a couple of hours, and then he had to return it. But taking a ride was fantastic. The whole neighborhood was looking, and I felt like royalty. It was redemption for all of those embarrassing years. With its return to the dealer, we thought the excitement was short-lived but to our unbelievable shock, he brought home a '59 Bird...identical...same color, same everything. Now we were sure he was finally either breaking out or having a breakdown! We didn't know which and didn't much care. We loved the new Lou!

Chapter Thirteen
DAD'S 88

Enter Tommy Crawford. Tommy was the son of our parent's best friends and held maybe the best job in the world, being the General Manager of our local VW dealership. That was like having a cousin work for the Orioles…you knew someone in a very high place! Come to find out, this was the source of these spectacular cars. For Tommy, it came naturally. Duarte Crawford, his Dad, had fueled our car fantasies by being the only adult we knew who could buy a new Cadillac every other year. As our Dad's friend, we would occasionally ride in these incredible vehicles, starting with his iconic '59 Caddy Sedan de Ville, whose outrageous fins finally surpassed Chrysler in the flamboyant '50s fin war! (Did you know the fin craze was started by GM's Harley Earl, after his design team saw a P-38 lightening warplane and incorporated the first fins on the 1948 Cadillac? And did you know the 1959 Cadillac had to be designed

around Buick front doors because the retooling cost
was too great. It was quite the challenge).

Anyway, Mr. Crawford's sky blue (Magic Mirror
Acrylic Lacquer finish, as it was known) four door
hardtop de Ville was a magnificent creation and was
my introduction to car air conditioning, power windows, 3-way power seats, 2-speed wipers, and an
"Autronic" high beam dimmer. We marveled over
the Wonderbar radio and the sound emanating from
an optional rear speaker (at a pricey $165. You can
get a digital CD DVD player and speakers for that
today!). One forgets that even outside rearview mirrors were optional, as were the now commonplace
back-up lights! If wealth were determined by how
much chrome was in the grille, particularly from the
hundred plus jewel like grille inserts, the Crawford's
were millionaires. Under the hood lived a 390 cu.
in. famous Cadillac motor, a Carter AFB four barrel developing 325 ponies channeled through a GM
Hydra-Matic. This car even had "cruise control," a
$97 option, and that had to be explained to me sev-
eral times..."You mean it drives itself?"

So Tommy running a dealership also meant an
inside track for my car crazy brother to snag a job as
a lot boy. And it was Tommy who convinced Brother
Doug to convince the altered state Lou Piersant that
we needed the prettiest 1959 Dynamic 88 Oldsmobile convertible in all of Baltimore. Shoot...after Dad
tasted champagne with those two T-Birds, he was
primed to buy this Olds. Like classic drug dealers,

those boys knew exactly what they were doing to Lou. There was no getting out of it!

I remember him coming home and announcing that everyone needed to come outside to see what he "bought!" "Bought??" My sister and I raced together through the door onto the porch, and there on the street sat a long shiny red monster with a white convertible top. You can't imagine our disbelief. Was he toying with us again? With the "Come on!" and "You have got to be kidding" out of the way, we surveyed every inch of this amazing behemoth, bumper to bumper. What an Amercian machine! Bright red with a  white top, red vinyl interior with 5" wide white accent strips around the edges of the long bench seats. It had red and white trimmed door panels, a two-tone, red over white dash; and this amazingly thin steering wheel, delicately attached to a deep "V" flanked by slender chrome shifter and blinker stalks. It was total Flash Gordon. The dash instrument cluster and matching indented glove box section were tied together by a ribbon of chrome and radio.

Dad popped the hood and there sat a giant 371 Cube, 270 horse Rocket V8. The hubcaps were ribbed chrome saucers, each sporting a three spoke spinner in the middle and accents of matching red behind the spinners and between the ribs. And the white walls were three slender concentric rings. The fat white wall in general had been giving way to more slender rings over the previous three years, but THIS was three slender rings together...how cool! We were disbelieving of this entire thing! Later I discovered that the "Super 88" and, of course, luxurious "98" were its big brothers, sporting standard 394 cube, 315 horse power plants. And of course, its sister car, the Pontiac Bonneville, could be optioned with the Holy Grail - 389 cubic engine with three deuces, producing an amazing 348 horses! But I didn't care. We didn't have power windows or seats, and just had a standard pushbutton radio, but this was a Hydra-Matic OLDS, and a convertible no less!

Although not ahead, I think we were finally "in the pack" in the neighborhood one-upsmanship competition. The Ruters had a dark green '59 Bonneville, two door hardtop. And the Fitzells (Mr. was a high school principal) had a frost green 1959 Buick, four door. These were our car's first cousins (all GM shared the B body in 1959), and all three had so many similarities that it was easy to tell GM was trying to save money (now there's an oxymoron!) But our car was fabulously beautiful, and the clear "cool department" winner! I later learned that the designers called this Olds body the "linear look" with the subdued tail fin lines starting at the front bumper, under two chrome rocket ornaments and tracing all the way to the rear lights. The massively wide grilled projected the name "OLSMOBILE" in neatly spaced

block letters separating dual, wide (and, after reflect-
ing, really ugly) headlight pods.

Dad powered the top back over our heads, into
a cavernous, black linen-lined well. The first-time
thrill of watching metal straps pivot and fold into
place and the top bending in sections over our head
was magic. I recall Dad halting the operation and
laying a towel across the back window as it creased,
saying something about being instructed to do this
so the window wouldn't scratch. Then from the trunk
Dad produced a matching red vinyl boot (this is
where I learned the term "boot!") which Cheryl and I
were quickly taught to snap into place from our spots
in the back seat. Dad proudly climbed in with Mom
as passenger (Doug must have been working) found
the right new key, and turned over the big Rocket
V8. As we pulled from the curb, Dad directed our
attention to the speedometer and said, "Watch this!"
To our utter fascination, a ribbon inched across the
speedometer's 20 inch wide face, left to right, chang-
ing colors from green to red as we sped up. What will
they think of next? Its narrow and quite hip three
ring white wall tires and spinner hubcaps added to
its outstanding stature as a road king. Here we were,
tooling along in a beautiful Olds, top down, smelling
the air and living the American dream.

Chapter Fourteen

WHAT HAPPENS WHEN YOU'RE FINALLY COOL!

There was a fifties decade Oldsmobile motto, "Make a Date with a Rocket 88!" We not only dated; we were happily married to our "88"! That Olds was a family member for five years. Its tenure coincided with my brother's first date, visits to TDI (Timonium Drive In), cruises through Ameches (yes, that Alan Ameche, the Colt's "Horse" who owned a Drive-In), drag races under my brother's care, and rides to the ice cream shack on hot summer nights. Cheryl remembers driving it to school in 1965, her senior year.

While interviewing my brother about the car, he remembered he and Rick taking on a' 62 bubble top Impala Chevy. They pulled up to a light together, Doug noting that the Chevy had a radical cam lope, and the always mischievous Rick asked the '62's driver if he wanted to run. Doug said, "I told Rick to shut up, but it was too late." The light changed, and the Chevy pulled a hole shot. Doug nailed it and the drag was on, until a Baltimore County cop passed in the opposite lane, threw on his single red roof light and started his u-turn. Thinking quickly (which Doug had to do often when Rick was involved), he turned right into a subdivision, killed the lights and crept through the streets in the dark for half a block. Not feeling the least bit safe, he then made a split-second decision to borrow an unused open garage of a complete stranger's house. Pulling in and killing the engine, he remembers Rick saying to him, "Boy isn't this a stroke of luck, you knowing these people on this street!" Doug said, "I don't know these people, and keep your voice down!" He recalls they sat for fifteen minutes, then took the back roads home.

THIS was one spectacular looking car in 1959! So much so that it was stolen one night. It had given us much joy, but now was giving some thief an equal amount. We all couldn't believe anyone would be dumb enough to steal a car that was this obvious! It was giant, red, and clearly unmistakable. Sure enough, the police found it a week later and returned our prized family member. But she was, in all honesty, getting a little long in the tooth. Here it was 1964, and the white convertible top wasn't so white anymore. Dad had been through several back window replacements, and the red paint was oxidizing to a nice pink color. He was getting the itch, we could tell, particularly when he brought home a 1962 T-Bird...the man really wanted a T-Bird! This model had the swivel steering wheel and the sequential taillights, but he didn't pull the trigger and kept on driving the old Olds. And I'm sure by this point the reader can determine that I had some pretty significant sensory overload with this car!

Chapter Fifteen
ADD A DASH OF MOTORCYCLE

As if I didn't have enough combustion engine confusion at age twelve, Doug started talking about motorcycles. This was generally a taboo topic around the parents, with comments from them like, "over my dead body" and "when hell freezes over," but, of course, that didn't deter Doug. His pals were going through a Vespa motor scooter phase, and Doug had to get in on it. So, with the house divided, Doug proceeded to explore the two wheel world with me tagging along. We weren't complete strangers to motorbikes. The man who previously owned the Hueback house had a full dress red Harley which he kept hidden in the garage. I recall him sneaking it out a few times before he moved. It apparently influenced me to the degree that I thought I should become a motorcycle cop. I stayed on that kick until I was out of high school and actually picked up a Baltimore City Police Academy application! It must have *REALLY* affected me. And then there was some guy who lived two bocks down and owned a black 900 Harley Sportster. He'd drive by frequently, and Jimmy and I would always comment on its wasp like, mean looks and its thunderous straight pipe sound!

But hot motorcycles were not going to be our downfall. Being that brother Doug was a folk music, button down collar preppy kind of guy, scooters were in order. But to be different, which he refined to an art, he decided on a Honda "50" instead of the Vespa. Why? It was the latest thing; wheels like a motor-cycle, a banana seat, hydraulic clutch, and relatively peppy for 50 c.c. scooter. And maybe most important, they were dirt cheap! I'll never know how he did it, but he first talked the parents into letting him buy the thing. THAT alone was amazing. But more incredible, he talked them into letting me ride on it!

Before I finish this story, I have to pay tribute to Pete's Cycle Shop. Pete established his store in the precinct called Hamilton. As one traveled south on Hartford Road, he would pass through Parkville on his way to Hamilton, three long walking miles from our house, and given that equal distance again, would find himself in the heart of Baltimore City. It was our single greatest adventure; walking all the way to

Hamilton on a Saturday. Pete's would be the extreme limit of our travel or the point of no return (being on the far side of Hamilton!). It was enough to say we did it and always a bonus to drink in the exotic British motorcycle inventory and fabulous smells. I mean how cool was it to own a motorcycle shop? I was permanently corrupted from the first visit; the magnetism of gasoline, leather, rubber, plastic and paint smells emanating from the most rebellious vehicles on earth. Pete was a BSA, Honda, and Vespa dealer, and for us junior motorheads, we were instantly addicted.

So, through some momentary and horrible lapse in judgment from my parents, I found myself sitting on the back of that white banana seat, fists gripping the passenger strap, feet on the fold down foot pegs, taking my first motorcycle/scooter ride. Doug climbed aboard, turned his head back to me to see if I was both comfortable and ready, then said, "Lean when I lean!" It never occurred to me that he hardly knew how to ride the thing by himself, much less with a passenger on board. But this was my big brother. He would never put me in danger, would he? Not being too bright, I had conveniently forgotten that this was the same boy who had taken his ten year old kid brother on a suicide run in a '55 Chevy!

Oh well, we were off, and the immediate sensation was exhilarating; balance, wind, power, and control. Doug headed up our relatively safe Willoughby Road, up shifting and steady as a rock. Remember, this was pre-helmet days, so I was riding as if this was a bicycle and I was a passenger on the handlebars (which, come to think of it, was never safe either!). The only accessory was Doug's very cool blue tinted goggles. We came to a stop without drama and prepared to enter the main thoroughfare of Hartford. This was going to be the real test. Negotiating traffic hadn't occurred to me, and I felt the uptick of anxiety. Here we go! Doug pulled out and accelerated nicely, stayed with traffic and showed off the spunk of this little red Honda. Okay, I was starting to get the hang of it. We'd lean left and right to change lanes, and I felt like a participant rather than a passenger. All was going swimmingly until we encountered the need to switch lanes over the dreaded street car ruts (buried rails). Baltimore had done away with streetcars in the early '50s, but hadn't gotten around to repaving the concrete streets. Those pesky parallel rail troughs lined the road all the way into the city.

And so, Doug didn't quite hit the groove at a sharp enough perpendicular angle, and the skinny tires of the Honda 50 wedged perfectly into one of those steel troughs. Heck, we all knew from our bicycle riding how to run over the things, but with these broader tires maybe you didn't have to worry... whatever Doug's previous experience (I was think-ing "none"), we were in a heap of trouble. The good news was that we didn't go down. The bad news was we did everything but go down. We lost all steering as the wheels and trough took control. And it was simply by the grace of God that we didn't simultaneously face plant. It must have been one of those "Oh no!!" moments for eye witnesses. The little Honda lodged yet kept rolling, and in an attempt to drive us out of the rut, it threw us left, then hard right, then hard left again. Recovery came from some hasty, high speed footwork and sheer brute force. We quickly retired to the side of the road to regain a morsel of composure. I recall we had a united sense of dodging the BIG bullet! Doug's line was, "I saved us!" "Yeah, way to go, Doug! What about the part where you almost killed us?" I said. Of course, Doug's next line was, you guessed it… "Do NOT tell Mom and Dad!" Okay, the third near death experience was now out of the way! Doug went on to have a few nice wrecks on the thing, thankfully without me.

Finally, Doug pulled a Buddy Messick with Wayne Kempskis brand new Vespa 125. Wayne had less than ten miles on his new scooter, for which he had saved every dime for two years. He dropped by the house and invited Doug to "take her for a spin!" My brother didn't make it to the Poteet's house before he dropped it on some black ice, thoroughly destroying the right side of Wayne's brand new ride. It also left Doug with permanent scars on his arm, still visible now fifty years later. Wayne wasn't a happy camper, and it took Doug two summers to pay him back for the repairs. There was just something about showing off new two wheelers on Willoughby Road! They should have posted a sign!

But Doug got the motorcycle thing out of his system. I, unfortunately, did not and have owned a few of bikes over the years. Any youthful indiscretions Doug may have exhibited back then, I more than doubled. I just tried not to repeat his!

Chapter Sixteen
WE'RE MOVING?

It was a most traumatic announcement! "We're moving!" "We're moving??" "Yes, we're moving!"

I had spent my first thirteen years in Parkville. When they use the term "formative" mine seemed more seminal! This was my home. It was where my friends lived and where we had perfected the places where we played and conquered every bike riding obstacle. My schools and our church were within walking distance, and Double Rock was our own amusement park. We had mastered its hiking trails and rock formations (way before there were climbing walls!). I had accumulated a small fortune in models and toys. Our music careers were blooming, and the Heubecks had finally entered the car extravaganza when Carol's boyfriend bought a TR2. I was king of my well-oiled domain! We're leaving this?

The year was 1964. I was in the seventh grade, having graduated from my cozy elementary school next door to the junior high. We could still walk to the new school, but now I found it more convenient to reach by bike. This was where, while in morning science class, I was informed that John Kennedy had been assassinated. Brother Doug had gone off to college, causing a significant shift in the attention I received. Cheryl was finishing high school and had a great steady boyfriend. Mr. Zitnick had finally let me play accordion with his Polka band at weddings. Mr. Fitzell had been made principal of Perry Hall Junior High School, and his son Danny had amassed a gun collection envied by the gun professionals everywhere. Yes, there had been the few unexpected pregnancies and shotgun weddings; odds favored such events with eighteen boys in the neighborhood. And there had been the arguments heard through open windows and car accidents that led to speculation about too much drinking. But, we were an American neighborhood, and, for me, things had matured nicely at 3018 Willoughby Road. I was being taken from all of this?

Apparently so! Dad had been mercifully lifted off night shift; promoted to a middle management position at the paper. It was an important break for him, for he had worked tirelessly for this recognition, and his value was finally being rewarded! Dad was no slouch when it came to work, work ethic and practical sense. We all knew that he was right far more often than wrong. So with career affirmation under his belt, he and Mom decided it was time to "move on up!" Unbeknownst to us kids, they had been looking at houses in the Dulaney Valley area of Maryland.

This section of Baltimore was where the "really nice" houses were. It was our equivalent to Palm Springs. Once you crossed into the neighborhood, you felt self conscious about what you were wearing. It also was where many of my Heros lived, like Johnny Unitus and Brooks Robinson. The parents had apparently found a new subdivision with "medium" priced homes, but with all the amenities of the more expensive cribs: three and four bedrooms, two and a half baths, dens, fireplaces, nice yards; the works! Dad felt we deserved better than a flooding basement and a partially finished second story, so he plunked down his money and off we went!

We moved during the end of summer 1964, me kicking and screaming all the way. I remember how miserable I made Mom and Dad that year. They thought they had ruined my life, and I didn't let them believe otherwise. I couldn't help myself! Dulaney Valley was a strange place full of strange people of a higher class breeding, and I was a street smart city boy, plain and simple. I made Mom and Dad promise to take me back to Parkville whenever I felt the need, and they were better than their word. Jimmy's parents opened their house to me, and I practically lived there every weekend for the next three years.

So what does this have to do with cars? Actually, these could be considered my independence days. With hotrods no longer coming to the house, and no license of my own, I had to improvise. At thirteen,

I went looking for those who could drive to get my kicks. Remember my neighbor Joey Clover? Joey was sixteen, just three years older, and the Clovers still had that beautiful yet proportionally odd shaped '59 Galaxy with the retractable roof. Joey was the first of our "closer in age" friends to start driving, and we had prearranged to cruise the boulevards with him the minute he had his license! I was at Jim's house and still can't recall the reason he couldn't go, but I was picked up by Joey and off we drove, top tucked in the trunk, feeling like "the man!"

It was a pretty funny start. Joey showed up wearing these black wraparound sunglasses, a pack of cigarettes rolled in his white t-shirt sleeve, and looked every bit the part of James Dean. This guy had just gotten his license and was already deep into the part! Even funnier, it was getting dark and those shades were useless, but they weren't coming off. He was way cool! And although I thought I was tough stuff too, I was still just a kid and acted like one. The evening turned into the Mutt and Jeff routine. I was asking nonstop questions like, "Where we goin, Joe? Huh, Joe? Where we headin??" Think we'll get there soon, Joe?" "Boy, Joe, you're a really neat guy, Joe!" He, on the other hand, didn't volley back five words in what became a one-sided conversation the entire night. But we cruised Amchees and all over Parkville and Hamilton, and it was a glorious evening for us. I think Joe realized quickly I was still too young for the likes of him, but it didn't matter. If we could persuade him to take us on the occasional ride, Jim and I were as close as we could get to having our own wheels!

And Joey had the car touch (or Willoughby fever). He actually did know what was cool as evidenced by his first car purchase. We weren't sure where the money came from, but he showed up one day in this awesome sky blue 1964 Chevelle Malibu Super Sport hardtop with white interior, 283 cubic inch engine, bucket seats, console, built in tachometer, and a stout looking chrome four speed. Oh my goodness! We were gonna not only cruise in style, we now had some muscle! Granted, it was a little underpowered, but the small block with a four barrel and duals was alive with rumble and personality, and the Borg Warner tranny mated to the M21 close ratio four speed made the coolest  whine between shifts. We all learned to add sound effects of a car running through the gears whenever we were recounting a good car story, and I can still imitate that winding sound mixed with an appropriate amount of V-8 rumble!

And being underpowered (220 horses) didn't last long. Over the next three years, Joey got real serious with the SS, adding a dual quad intake manifold off a Corvette, a set of Headman headers, and dressed it off with chrome Keystone mags. Now it was REALLY nice looking! He later claimed it was cammed up with an Isky (to take all that gas from twin fours). These tweaks continued on that Chevelle long after I got my license and the Malibu ended up being a dragster of sorts; no front wheel wells, skinny front tires, Sun tach, the whole enchilada!

During those three conflicted years, some pretty darn good things happened! Although I wouldn't admit it, I was growing more accustomed to our new digs in Timonium (that's the official town of Dulaney Valley). The schools were huge, ultra modern places, highly rated academically and known for their sports domination. I discovered that the majority of the Orioles and Colts kids went to our schools, and athletes were as numerous as freckles on a redhead. I had not made any friends half way through the eighth grade and was coming down a stairwell between classes at Ridgely Junior High, a particularly gigantic school, when the guy in front of me said to his buddy, "Let's find a place to sneak a smoke!" Then some guy behind me leaned over my shoulder and asked, "You don't smoke do you?" "Na, do you?" "Na!" That brief conversation led to a lifelong friendship with my then newest, now my oldest friend, Dan Sutphen. Danny was a big blonde guy with a friendly face and a warm presence, and I knew he could easily be my pal. We went on to have many adventures together, some of them too wild to capture in this book. You'll hear more about Dan, but he was one of my "bridge" friends between my old life and new one.

Also, towards the end of these three years, the muscle car era was getting into full swing. On February 2, 1962, a man named Carroll Shelby, famous for his late '50s European racing of Ferraris and Maseratis, shoehorned a 260 Ford engine into a '62 AC Bristol (shipped from its English manufacturer sans engine and transmission), and with the addition of a four speed Borg Warner tranny later that day, the AC Cobra was born. Later that year, and with the very aggressive but low profile help of Ford motor company, Shelby America was also hatched. The first official Cobra was CSX 2000 and eventually 125 were built so that the little aluminum car could officially race the Corvettes and Ferraris it was designed to beat. In 1963, with a one ton weight advantage, it started knocking off Stingrays on the track. Imitation is the sincerest form of flattery and Ian Garrad begins cramming 260s in Sunbeam Alpines and calling them Tigers. Shelby eventually took these over and built them in his shop.

In was in that same year when Shelby and company upped the ante and wedged a 427 into CSX 2166 to beat the Ferrari GTO in Sebring Florida. It went on Ferraris' home turf, and won the 24 Hours of Lemans! If Carroll hadn't cemented our vote for hotrod king, he did when his company introduced the GT 40! We went wild. These rapid

advancements were making us delirious! There was
no stopping this crazy man named Shelby and his
legend was being solidified with each car built and
race won. My Uncle Jimmy bought a new 1964 Red
Mustang with a white roof and a 260 cubic inch V-8.
You could sense it was somehow connected to this
entire Shelby/Ford racing mentality, and its popular-
ity would prove every owner wanted "in" on the fun.
The Mustang was radically different; sporty, compact
and youthful!

As if to draw them out in the open, Shelby introduced the 350 GT Mustangs in late '64, making the
connection to Ford forever undeniable. This was
a high performance fast back designed to compete
against Corvettes in the SCCA-B class to Chevy's
great consternation. Enzo Ferrari was fed up and
withdrew from 1965 FIA racing. Between the iconic
Cobra Daytona, regular Cobras, the GT 40 and the
350 GTs, Shelby owned the race tracks. Drivers
named Phil Hill, Bob Bondurant, Allen Grant, Bob
Holbert, Bill Krause, Dave McDonald, Ken Miles,
Dan Gurney, Jo Schlesser, Harold Keck, and car
designer Pete Brock became gearhead idols. Hertz
even started renting 350 GT's for the average Joe to
experience. The stories around that wonderfully, ill-
fated fiasco would take another book.

I discovered during these three years one other
jewel! On the north end of Parkville we had a
Chrysler Plymouth dealer named Doug Griffth, and
he added to his inventory a couple of little fiberglass

cars named Griffth 200s. We, of course, thought these were his creation since they appeared to have his name, but, coincidentally, it wasn't the case. Since there was no shortage of people attempting to best Carroll Shelby, the Griffth was in an English TVR... AC Bristols were already taken! Mark Donohue and Gerry Sagerman had driven a TVR Grantura at Sebring in 1962. Jack Griffth, convinced the Blackpool based company to send him TVRs Grantura's chasises without an engine and transmission (much like Carroll had done with Bristol) They eagerly agreed, no doubt dreaming of a similar success as Bristol had. Griffth proceeded to stuff Ford 289 V-8s into the engine bays. Reportedly, he made 192 of them. In 1965, the advertised price of this 1,450 pound baby rocket was $3,995. It was claimed that Cobra were breaking the 4 second 0-60 m.p.h. mark, and the little Griffth with a high performance 289/271 horsepower engine was said to equal that performance with a 3.9 second record. So here, in my town, was an outlet to buy Cobra beaters. There was always a story when it came to trying to outdo the fastest car on the planet.

But with all of these things happening, my time in Parkville was coming to a close. Joey and I had gone our separate ways. He caught on to our schemes and started hanging with people his own age. But his contribution to my adolescence and car habits was considerable. Dave Class introduced me to the Corvair. He had a maroon "Monza" with a white convertible top. He later bought a 1964 Monza "Spyder" with an aluminum, horizontally opposed six cylinder 150 horse turbocharged engine. A few other cars were still in the neighborhood, including a '65 Super Sport Impala at the Poteets, but most of the excitement was over and it was time for me to start my life for real in Timonium.

Those three painful years were filled with not so painful memories. If the truth be told, I found many ways to be happy. In retrospect, I was growing up and life for a thirteen-year-old boy is excoriating. It's worse for the parents. I put Mom and Dad through things they did not deserve. Had they seen my face when playing music at the coffee house or cruising the boulevards with Joey, they would have said, "You're sandbagging us, son!" I was. I'm afraid I didn't make up for it once I got my license. That's the next story!

PART TWO
1966 TO 1971
"Look Mom, I'm driving!"

Chapter Seventeen
"WHERE IT STARTED…"

It was summer in Baltimore, 1967. My new friend, Wally, had just banged on our front door and was standing on the porch, Paul McCartney hair, hands thrust in his jean pockets, with his father's new Forrest Green Cougar GT on the street just over his shoulder. I brushed him back with the swing of the screen door, bounding down the steps, barely hearing him as he chased me to the passanger door. His words started sinking in when I heard, "It's Dad's!" implying that since his father worked for a clandes-

tine division of Ford racing, this was no ordinary GT. Leaning hard on the roof, arms supported above the window in the "arrest/pat down" position, head ducked, staring in, I said, "Let's go!" (actually, he was already around to the drivers side, jumping in). I raked the door handle and in a liquid motion was next to him. He didn't need to say it as we both grabbed our lap belts, rare in the '60s, but a natural instinct and respect for the rocket we were about ride.

Living in the "burbs", on a wide asphalt road and the beginning of a half mile slightly downhill straight away (on a route directly one mile from high school) guaranteed the best, and simultaneously most complained about, drag strip in the county. It actually succumbed to speed bumps as early as 1980 (far before that was fashionable too), an indication of just how "find me first gear quick" inviting EastRidge Road was!

Walley twisted the key, and the hydraulic lifter 390 sprang to life through, what he deemed, "factory headers" running under my feet. Is that a cam lope I hear? I recall a lump in my throat as he inched away from the curb. I broke the revere with a side glance and a comment, "Automatic?" I don't remember an answer as he mashed the accelerator. I was G-forced back into my seat, my elbows helplessly swinging past my sides, pointing to the rear window. In an instant, 5,000 rpms exploded into a cloud of blue tire smoke and two posi-perfect black stripes, which adorned my street and remained there like embarrassing tatooes for literally months! I recall a fleeting thought, "My parents are gonna flip-out!!" since this would make the umteenth time THAT had happened!

But I digress...Here I was, crushed into the passanger seat of one of maybe the quickest street cars

I'd ever ridden in, surpressing a scream. I recall it
getting no traction through two of its three up shifts.
Wally was doing the left-right steering wheel jerk to
keep the long Green nose pointed, the 390 howling
in the high key of "E," and then throttling back just
to start finding traction. As my neighbors houses
blurred, I calculated the distance to the stop sign and
wondered just how crazy my old buddy was. But
he started braking hard 50 yards from the stop sign
and once stopped, he casually said "and disc brakes
too," to which I forced a nervous, " Holy mother of
earth!!!" He looked both ways, eased left onto Potsprings Road (another straighaway) and halfway into
the turn nailed it again, torquing the backend out
voliently and countering with a couple of opposite
lightening cranks on the steering wheel to straighten
up. Then he lifted, the nose dived and we immediately transformed into a civilized cruiser.

Wally said, "Like it?" "Are you kidding me?" I
said. He launched into a bunch of facts about having
something north of 380 BHP (from a normal factory 335), a special 3:90 rear, a C6 automatic and that
his Dad's co-workers couldn't wait to put this one on
the street. It was then time for another accelerator
mashing demonstration as if to confirm Wally's fresh
description. As the Ford big block tached up to a
glorious roar, side street and trees blurred and my fear
and exhillaration broke into wild laughter. This sleeper
was gonna make high school history because I knew its
DNA was otherworldly and it was being proven!

Just think about, who had a Dad who could create something this hot? Beyond checking the "GT Performance Group" box, he apparently had the clout to make a few calls and twist a few arms. Although he ranked as the coolest father that year, I questioned his sanity for letting (frequently) a couple of 17-year-old apes trash the new Firestone F-70s. Of course, I always questioned his son's sanity! With every toss of the keys from father to son, Wally would turn up at my house for the next thrill ride. It was like getting high together! And we'd run at any stop light, against any comer, and frequently blew the doors off of many otherwise surprised big block gods. Wasn't a Cougar suppose to be an upscale Mustang with medium power? Not this one! It became a legend in our circles and remained one of the strongest street performers in my muscle car history.

Chapter Eighteen
BEETLES AND BEATLES

Alright, so I wasn't as miserable as I was pretend-ing to be! Timonium was, let's just say, improving. As my whining subsided, Mom and Dad had a glim-mer of hope that I had turned the corner. I was visit-ing the old neighborhood less and lingering longer in our new one as new friendships and hang-outs grew more familiar and trusted. Much like a good pair of jeans, you hated the new ones but you had to wear 'em in order to make 'em old ones! The house was becoming "my home," aided by my parents' bribe to let me freely decorate my room. It was a weak-kneed strategy, but it worked. And I wasn't shy. By the age of sixteen, the entire room, walls and ceilings, were subliminal messages painted in wild, dayglow paint using all kinds of psychedelic themes, shapes, and forms. I had commandeered our older RCA console stereo (it too had a detachable speaker) and blared the Moody Blues "Nights in White Satin," Iron But-terfly's "IngoDadavida," and, of course, any of the

Beatles whenever I was "in residence!" The Eastridge house was a split foyer job and my bedroom was at the far end of the hall, just inches from my parent's room. I, therefore, had my eye on a downstairs bedroom from day one.

There were several houses similar to ours on our street. Ours was billed as the "Colonial Model" with barn-yard red shingles, white trim, black shutters, a multi- paned picture window (our first), a brick foundation (the brick supposedly from the old Ford Theater) and four two-story white columns encasing the centered front door. It didn't have the character and broken-in glove feel of my Willoughby home, but it was a better house, heated and even air conditioned. My mind eventually accepted, and my body certainly cheered the modern amenities and softer living. If I was going to live in Dulaney Valley, this was as good a place as any.

From 1964 to 1966 (the year of my license), my new friend, Dan, greatly eased the transition. Interestingly, his house was halfway between Parkville and our new one. How apropos! And his place was way cool! He lived in the country in a big house nestled in the middle of a gentleman's farm, surrounded by some serious working farms. He was the oldest of five, and his home was always full of people and laughter, fun and freedoms. As I've said, Dan and I had some outrageous experiences together, many of which aren't suitable for reprint, but he also was a car freak, and I'm free to write about most of those escapades.

Of course, every kid remembers the day he got his license. I sure do. Several years before "officially" having my permit, I had accumulated hours of driving. Whether it was driveways or country roads, I would wrangle the driver's seat away from sympathetic elders at any opportunity. You'd be surprised how often I was allowed to drive. Were these people crazy? Doug had left college, joined the Air Force and was stationed stateside. When he'd visit, he would bring home his very conservative and new poor man's Porsche, the 1966 white 1300 VW Beetle. Big brother would let me drive it as often as I'd ask. I recall it came naturally and I wasn't the least bit nervous to take up the clutch and drive off. After that, I acted like a veteran with increasing smoothness with every exploit.

Whatever Doug drove, the rest of the family mimicked. Cheryl bought a Beige 1300 VW and Dad bought "the house" (which was code for my car), a 1959 VW. Hotrods were very much alive in our friends' garages, but the Piersants were taking a collective horsepower break. Here we were driving three bugs. And my July 1966 driver exam with that VW will never be forgotten. The house VW had a broken passenger seat. Its backrest was permanently reclined at about 45 degrees. Back then the Department of Motor Vehicles annex was at the police station in Bel Air (pronounced

"Blair" by Baltimo-rons) so a Baltimore County cop rode shotgun as my examiner. He obviously wasn't their premiere police officer, having been relegated to riding shotgun with snot-nosed sixteen-year-olds. It may have had something to do with his physical fitness as he was as round as he was tall. That made for a comical sight when he eased himself into my passenger seat and leaned back. He immediately realized that he was staring at my dash board, leisurely reclining a foot behind me. The disgust instantly registered on his face, and I knew I had better nail this driving and the dreaded parallel parking feat without blemish. I remember him waddling his body back and forth to gain a more upright position and ended up with his butt wedged half way up on the seat back just to get a clear view out of the windshield. Even I was embarrassed for him. Ignoring the sweat in my eyes, I started my rehearsed maneuvers. He barked instructions, while simultaneously looking down and around at his seat, trying to assess the chances of a better, more natural looking sitting position. I was flawless, thank the Lord, and as he opened the door to exit, he looked back over his shoulder at me and said, "You passed...and get this seat fixed, will ya?"

VWs were the "other white meat" revolution of the '50s and '60s. If America was to have a foreign car, it wanted one it could rely on. Once we discovered we could trust Volkswagon, we embraced it as the "only" acceptable foreign car option until Datsun and Toyota muscled their way in. Designed largely

by Dr. Porsche, the company was founded in Nazi
Germany in 1937 as the "People's Car"(the transla-
tion for Volkswagen). Two cars were eventually
sold in America in 1949, marketed as the "Victory
Wagon." The famous split rear window went away
in 1953 in favor of a solid oval window and then a
rectangle one in 1957. Imports dribbled in, but over
30,000 were registered in the states by 1955, when
Volkswagon of America was formed. Between 1955
and 1960 another 160,000 were registered. Mine was
a blue '59, with an 1191 c.c. (the 1200) 32 horsepower engine, and a reserve gas tank instead of a gas
gauge! Since gas was 31 cents a gallon, I'd put in
$2 worth, drive for five days, run out of gas, flip the
reserve tank lever with my big toe (it was to the right
of my gas pedal) and drive for another two days!

My bug became a trusted and highly abused
companion. I eventually painted the hood and trunk
inserts Dayglow orange. And we discovered you
could reverse the wheels, put 'em back on and they'd
stick out to the edge of the fender, looking every
bit like deep dish mags. Those I painted Dayglow
yellow (I know what you're thinking…but this *was*
the '60s…). I cropped the shifter down to about
four inches tall, and not being an attentive shop class
student, found that I couldn't re-tap the threads for
the huge chrome shift knob I had bought. So it just
rested and rattled on top of the stick. When my
first gear synchronizer stopped working, the shifter
would "POP' out of first gear mid-rev and that knob

would become an unguided missile, flying off and hitting either the back window or a passenger, whichever came first. Of course, I had finally opted for an Empi single throat muffler protruding from under the rear bumper, but only after a year of driving with the baffles removed from the original muffler. You could pull the engine and replace it in 60 minutes or less, and there was never anything that couldn't be repaired with a few bucks. It was the single cheapest and slowest car I'd ever own, but what could have been better for a sixteen-year-old?

We were a living VW commercial, which were great back then. Remember the Lemon commercial? When the family, friends and neighbors were all gathered at the house, we had eight VWs there! Doug, Cheryl and I each had one, my neighbor on the right had two, Dan Sutphen had a red and white VW bus, Dave Baker had a '64 Beetle convertible, and the neighbor across the street had one. It was hilarious! When I went on to marry my sweet wife, Suzanne, in 1975, maybe it was partially because she was driving a green VW bug!

Chapter Nineteen
"YOU WERE DRAG RACING?"

Although lightening fast, Walley's Cougar wouldn't be the quickest car I'd pilot. The VW *was*, though, the slowest! It was a great starter vehicle and allowed me to learn defensive driving skills. It was always the passee, never the passer (like flying a Piper Cub amongst the Blue Angels!). But it faithfully, albeit slowly, pulled the Eastridge Road hill up to my high school and regularly coasted back down it in the afternoons (to conserve gas, of course). It transported me to pick up dates or to cruise around with friends. It was barely basic transportation, but it was also commandeered as mine, and I was happy to have the wheels!

Thinking back on that period, my generation would prove as restless with its cars as it was with its government, the establishment and its war. Just how radical we could get, look and go would define our expectations. At sixteen, my hair began to grow (in more places than my head), my shirts got silkier, my bell bottoms wider, my music heavier, and my cars got faster (eventually). My school was a breeding ground for wealthy young kids to act out and play the fool. I was half in and half out of the "in" crowd, always remembering where I came from, the city streets of Baltimore. I wasn't afraid of a fight and wasn't a natural follower. To my surprise, that would eventually make me a leader. Preppies were everywhere at Dulaney High School, and since I wore penny loafers, imitating Doug and his friends; they assumed I was one as well. I kind of was, but the hair was growing and the clothes were, as Bob Dylan sang, "times were a changin'!" Remember, our generation executed a revolution, and every one of us were pioneers. In the car world, it seemed the Big Three had secret divisions who'd spy on kids and give us whatever wheels we could conjure in our minds.

But Japanese freighters were moored just off our shores, loaded with promising new cars and one such vehicle was the Datsun 1600. It was 1967. Doug had received orders for Germany and had shipped out. Cheryl landed a great secretarial gig at the local hospital and was ready to swap her 1300 VW for a sports car. Of course, the obvious choice was the MGB, with coaching from me. I could see myself driving it

more than her! As fate would have it, Nationwide Datsun had opened not three

miles from our house. They were advertising a new
little convertible sports car with a 1.6 L. motor and
twin SU carbs, producing 96 horses and an unheard
of 5 speed transmission! Wait a minute...that's one
more horse and one more gear than the MGB! What
were those Japanese up to?

With Dad's help, she brought home a red cabrio-
let Datsun 1600 with black interior and black convertible top. I examined it from bumper to bumper,
thinking that it wasn't quite as low as an MGB, and
maybe a little boxier, but it was muscular and fresh
looking. I determined that I liked it and, of course,
loved the whole idea of it. Excitedly, I climbed in
the passenger seat and noted a terrific looking leather
lined silver-grey dash, neatly arranged with quality
looking instruments, rows of toggle switches and a
three spoke steering wheel with aircraft machined
holes in each spoke. The wheel looked a little like
one from the fabulous Jag XKE. Nice touch, Japan!
The "Fairlady" as it was called in Japan, was quite
unique in that it had a cache of appointments that
would later distinguish most Japanese imports.
Cheryl was proud to give her little brother a ride,
but unlike my previous sibling jaunts, this time I
too could drive and was determined to get behind
that wheel! Quite naturally, I didn't expect it on the
maiden run. I was smoother than that. But it didn't
take a week before I was bugging the fool out of her
for the keys. I had had my license about a year and
when she finally relented, I profusely thanked her, ran

out, dropped the top and climbed in. Remember, I
had years of hotrod experience prior to this test drive,
but this was me driving our own (okay, Cheryl's)
unique sports car. I recall it just being dusk, and
I flipped the light toggle and watched an array of
instruments half way down the dash light up. It gave
an airplane cockpit sensation. I fired her off, studied
the shifter, engaged reverse, checked and adjusted the
mirrors and backed on to Eastridge Road. I cranked
the wheel to head down that straightaway Walley would so nicely deface in coming months, gave
opposing attention to the clutch and gas and slipped
off. My upshifts were met with strange new power
and a throaty engine note, and I immediately sensed
the pleasure this car could give. The new car smell,
the wind, the engine sounds, its sports car stance and
color, the aggressive interior; it was all very intoxicating.

I traveled through two more stop signs and joyfully repeated my upshift patterns from each. I
turned right onto Ridgely (fronted my old Junior
High) and made my way down to York Road, our
major thoroughfare. I waited patiently at the light,
blinker blinking, taking in the full ambience, the
evening air and this very cool car. Once green, I
turned left into the slow lane and traveled maybe 100
feet when an MGB surprised me, appearing to my
immediate left. Where had he come from? I was in
third gear about to shift, and I saw him nudge the
"B" forward, an aggressive leap that could only mean

one thing. I realized in an instant that I was about
to have my first, up close and personal drag race!
Forget the fact that I was in my sister's brand spanking new sports car (with temporary tags) during my
maiden, trust building voyage. This matchup was
too perfect to pass up. I downshifted to second and
we both slowed to equalize our speeds. Looking at
one another and back at the road, I waited for him to
make the first move, which he did. I responded with
full throttle and a hard upshift to third. We were
both tached up, ready for fourth, me edging him by a
half a car or so when the unthinkable happened. We
passed a hiding Baltimore police car, just like in the
movies. I'm not making this stuff up. The proof was
self evident when he pulled out like a rocket, roof
lights switched on. My knees turned to water and the
implications of what I had just done leapt into my
consciousness. Sure enough, regardless of my insanely
quick de-acceleration and instantly faked civilized
demeanor, he had me. I'd been in the car less than
ten minutes, and I was getting pulled over for drag
racing. Holy mother of trouble! Sure enough, he
picked me (not the MG...had to be the red color),
flashed his lights, and, in humiliation, I pulled into
a fast food parking lot, him hard on my tail. The
lecture was equally humiliating..."You've had this
car how long? What do you mean, it's not yours? Do
you know how fast you were going? How long have
you had your license, son? Do you want to keep your
license, son?"

Although I had been an aid in breaking the law since I was ten, this was my first professional criminal act. But heck, I could hardly be blamed. I'd been driving a 36 horsepower VW for a year. It couldn't muster 60 m.p.h. downhill. But there would be no mercy. The cop handed me a ticket for 70 in a 35 zone, $50 BUCKS (a fortune in 1967), accompanied by three points (in the new Maryland point system...five and you were dead meat!), and I still had yet to face the hangin judge when I returned home. Needless to say, that wasn't pretty. I recall sheepishly walking into the house, having determined on my very slow drive home that I'd isolate Mom, tell her first and then let the poison spread naturally to Cheryl. When the black news reached her, words still fail to describe her reaction. Let's just say, I didn't have to worry about driving her new Datsun again. The sliver lining was I didn't even have to worry about talking to her for a month either!

As expected, I was put on highly restrictive driving privileges and quickly put back in my Beetle so that no harm could possibly happen again. The VW had that effect! But I'd live to race again, and the speeds and stakes would be much higher. It's very hard to waste such a good lesson and I didn't. It made me smarter and wiser for the next race!

As a footnote, Cheryl wrecked that sweet little Datsun later that year. It was nighttime on an icy dark road, and she struck a flatbed trailer which was illegally sticking out of a driveway covering the entire left lane. To make matters worse, it had no reflectors on its side. It was a nasty accident, and Cheryl's life was spared by an act of God. Had she been several inches right or left, the consequences would have been horrific. The Datsun was never quite the same afterwards. The body shop had difficulty finding matching parts and the 1600 ended up have a '68 front fender and hood. The blush was off the rose!

Chapter Twenty
"OUR OWN PERSONAL RACE CAR!"

It started innocently enough for him. Doug was stationed in Zweibrucken Germany in 1965. His Air Force enlistment was turning out quite well as he had been moved into national security with a top secret clearance, giving him reasonable clout and long weekends to explore other pursuits. He and three of his Air Force buddies had taken an interest in weekend racing, mostly Formula One and Hill Climbs, and were visiting the various tracks around Europe as furloughs allowed. After a year of spectating, they found themselves in a bar discussing the merits of starting their own race team. The later the night, the more serious (or more drunk) they became. The pinnacle of their evening was a straw drawing event, where Doug drew the short one and was elected the driver. The other three would be the mechanics. Of course, they had to use *his* car! That wasn't exactly the winning straw!

A fellow by the name of Howard was a car dealer and would bring demos to the base for soldiers to drive, in hopes of a sale. Waving a new car under my brother's nose was akin to offering a banana to an ape...it was in his DNA to have it! So Howard sold Doug a new body styled 1967 Fiat 850, with 52 horses and a four speed. These were attractive little vehicles with their homeland Italian coach work and reasonable peppiness. The guys knew of an ex-patriot named Bill Vandeford who had quite a reputation for building fast Mini Coopers and racing them. The boys pooled their money, and Doug wrote home asking Mom and Dad to sell his life insurance policy (another happy conservation!) in an effort to let Bill perform his full magic on the Fiat. Doug was then sent to driving school, and they were in the weekend racing business!

Since they had decided to race in the Group II Touring Wagon class, there were strict rules applied to modifications of stock automobiles. With that understanding, Vandeford spent the next month blue printing and balancing the little 900 cc engine. He bored and honed the cylinders to perfect tolerances, indexed and nitrated the crank, installed a three-quarter Iskandary cam, jetted the two barrel carb (they weren't allowed to change or replace stock carburetion), and removed the front fender wells. He then designed, bent and installed one outrageous looking spaghetti header system, dual two-inch pipes that snaked away from the engine and exited together

just in front of the right rear tire He then beefed
the suspension and tires, stripped the interior to bare
metal, installed a racing seat, fire extinguisher and a
full roll-cage. With the application of a white competition stripe and large white circles for its numbers, the 850 was transformed into a 1,100 pound,
110 horsepower bona-fide race car. Bill broke in this
newly transformed sedan by racing it at the Nurbur-
gring, placing second in its class. He then handed
my brother the keys, assuring him it was lightening
quick and ready to compete!

Doug and Company took possession and began
their campaign, registering for races and trailering
the little Fiat all over Europe. He remembers the
thrill of competition and the highly addictive sensa-
tions of slinging a fire-breathing sports car around a
track, door to door with likeminded combatants in
hopes of a win. As a sixteen-year-old, I would listen
for news of his escapades and proudly, if not obnox-
iously, report on his progress to all my friends. (Rodger, would you please just shut up?) To me, it was all
glamour, and I was as proud as I could be. To Doug,
the momentary thrills were interrupted by days of
hard work…hectic weekends, unexpected and wallet-
emptying expenses, and largely losing results. Doug
and Company raced twelve times during the next
eighteen months, claiming fourth place as his best
performance. The band of brothers lost their zeal for
"participation," and Doug's racing career was over as
quickly as it started. It was all rather anti-climatic,

Doug recalls! Knowing that his military tour in
Germany was coming to an end as well, he decided
to ship the Fiat home. So in mid-year, 1968, the car
arrived at our house on Eastridge Road.

Although it was summer, it was Christmas for
me! Doug had been home for several weeks and was
acclimating to life stateside. His brief marriage to
his high school sweetheart had ended overseas, and
he was back to just being my big car crazed brother!
It would be a temporary situation, I knew, but I so
enjoyed his company again, and relished reliving
"the good old days." The blue racing car arrived
on a trailer on a Saturday morning. I bolted out to
the street and saw
for the first time in
person the car I'd only
seen in grainy black
and white photos.
Doug warned that
the battery may be low or drained completely. Once
unloaded, we didn't chance firing it off, pushed it up
the short driveway, engaged the parking brake, then
stood back to take a hard look at the famous visitor.
Doug was our tour guide, and I recall him leaning on
the car while Dad and I stood as his audience, listening to the transformation description while Doug
pointed and laughed at the various modifications and
battle scars. We stepped back as he reached in the
cockpit, disengaged the hood latch, and flipped open
the hood to reveal a tiny silver four cylinder engine,

accentuated by this dramatic spaghetti-like white header system, heavily browned at the exhaust mani-fold from heat. There was exceptional room under the hood with the fender wells missing, and sitting alone, the power plant looked dwarfed but fearsome. I walked the perimeter of the car and drank in its oversized racing numerals plastered on the doors and roof, its broad competition white stripe dividing the car bumper to bumper, matching white wheels, and two stout parallel exhaust pipes that exited out from under the side, singling it meant business!

"Okay, for heaven sakes start the darn thing!" I said. Doug climbed in, switched on an electric fuel pump (another indicator that this was no ordinary Fiat), and was greeted by silence, not the happy tapping of the little pump. Sure enough, when he turned the key there was an equal stillness. She was as dead as twelve o'clock! Without a battery charger, we considered jumping it off when Doug volunteered to go shopping for a new battery. Bringing the engine to life would have to wait, and the anticipation was killing me. So we ran to a local gas station, slapped down eleven bucks for a new battery and headed back to the house (yeah, eleven bucks…1968!). Dad had since disappeared, so Doug and I unloaded the old battery and replaced it with the new one (relocated to the trunk), attached the cables, and he climbed in the driver's seat for a second try. I was looking over his shoulder through the open door. He flipped the electric fuel pump switch and this time, it came on, clicking merrily. He let it run for five seconds and turned the key over to light up the dash, then looked over his left shoulder and encouraged me to back away from the straight pipes aimed directly at my shins. He cranked the starter. With a sudden cough, it awoke, a single flash of flames shooting from the exhaust, and an ear deafening 2,000 r.p.m. stacado.

"Gooood night, Miss Molley!" What a glorious sound! He burped the accelerator a few times and the little Fiat stumbled and missed. Doug yelled through the window, "She's not ready to run yet!" But his smile was infectious and while we waited, we enjoyed a Moment where our entire hotrod history was summed up in this one experience. The 850 settled into a rough idle, the cam lope obvious and the presentation about as lusty as you'd want from four inches of exhaust pipes openings. Confident she was ready, he revved the engine two or three times, the last a strong 6,000 r.p.m. sweep, and the escalating harmonic symphony of those four cylinders was thrilling and outrageous. And, it was so freakin loud, I couldn't believe that's what you had to listen to just below your left ear!

Of course, being about as street legal as a top-fuel dragster, the Fiat wasn't going anywhere. Or was it? Doug had that look in his eyes! Oh, man! Here we go! We hatched a plan to take it out the next morning, Sunday, when most everyone would be home, particularly the police. We would roll it from the garage, down the street far enough so that when it started, it would only sound like a fighter jet rather than a B-52! I tested a lawn chair in the passenger side and it kind-of worked, but mostly didn't. I would be taking my life in my hands but, hey, it wasn't the first time! And so the adventure was planned.

We crawled out of bed around eight Sunday morning, dressed quickly, and snuck past the parent's bedroom to the garage. I opened the door while Doug reached through the driver window and made sure it was in neutral. Stationed on both sides of the car, we shoved the light bodied 850 backward towards the street. Doug climbed in the driver seat, and I pushed from the passenger door. Since we were on a gentle slope toward Potsprings Road, there was little effort needed to get the Fiat rolling. We were maybe fifty yards from the house when Doug fired it off. I jumped in, landing in the lawn chair, which shifted and slid on the bare metal flooring. Like the day before, she wasn't ready to run and the 850 coughed and spat, stumbled and missed, while Doug feathered the accelerator to encourage her. We were in first gear, running about 20 miles per hour, the interior sound deafening; I'm sure waking and instantly irritating hundreds of people from their Sunday morning rest! And we hadn't even gotten on the thing yet! This was going to be bad and magnificent all at the same time!

The race car started to cooperate, and Doug was getting enough revs out of it to shift into second,

and coax the Fiat up to around 3,000 r.p.m.s for his
upshift to third. We would be at the stop sign in a
moment, so he dropped it back to neutral and let
her coast the balance of the way. The car still wasn't
ready to run, but with enough gas and clutch, we
eased across Potsprings and headed up the opposite
slope of Eastridge Road towards Ridgely Road. Doug
shouted, "It comes alive at 3,000 r.p.m.s. Get ready!"
I attempted to stabilize myself using feet and hands
on every flat surface I could find. Doug tached up to
around three grand again, shifted to second, stam-
mered back to three thousand, and then laid his foot
into it. The Fiat shot forward, wedging my seat
against the roll bar, forcing me to redouble my grip
on whatever it was I was holding. The engine Rs
climbed to 4,500 and that symphonic free revving
note and g-force took over, reminding us mortals that
this vehicle was transformed to romp! We were now
officially rattling "the Valley's" quiet Sunday morning revere and I was intoxicated. Doug upshifted and
moved towards the next stop sign where he matched
revs with down shifts and brought it to a halt. We
turned left onto Chamruth Road, a long, downhill
straightaway with a slow righthand sweeping turn at
the end. With the engine fully up to temperature,
Doug decided this was where he'd let it run. He
fully accelerated, and the tach effortlessly leaped to
redline. I had gained a pretty solid seat position and
was able to concentrate on the car rather than my
precarious perch. He shifted into second and wound

it out to red-line again, not letting the r.p.m.s drop below three thousand and keeping the little 900 c.c. engine in full power range. We were screaming down Charmruth when better judgment prevailed and he backed off (believe me, there was never an inkling of good judgment in any exercise Doug and I were involved in!). But he had accomplished the mission and effectively conveyed to me the thrill of driving in a race car. It was amazing how a small balanced engine could pull this 1,100 pound Go-Kart through the streets. The only thing left was to turn the wheel over to me ....which he did!

There was little of the experience that wasn't a rush. The clutch take up was easy, but the low track gearing caused me to stall about three times before I could ease away from a stop. Meanwhile, Doug was working on lodging himself in the lawn chair, a feat I'd mastered, and now it was his turn. Once I figured out the launch, I could feel the Fiats willingness to run above the magic three grand r.p.m. mark and its protests and stubbornness below it. It simply came alive in the power band. The handling was precise, the ride stiff and rough and there was no mistaking this car as some street poser. It may have been the original "tuner" car!

I had maybe fifteen minutes behind the wheel before we headed back to the house. The return trip was vaguely reminiscent of a drive home in the Datsun after my ticket. Doug and I were probably going to catch the full ire of the parents for ruining our family's reputation, disturbing the peace, and breaking at least ten major traffic laws, probably more. But I had Doug as my shield and, of course, he'd catch the brunt of it, with a few crumbs showering me. Surprisingly, and to our delight, Mom and Dad were past the point of embarrassment at our car shenanigans, and gave us the, "You really shouldn't have gone out there with that thing" speech and not much more. "That's all?" Were we making progress?

The Fiat didn't make any further encore exhibitions, and Doug sold it to a big-shot lawyer who promptly got busted for driving it on the streets. I'd say that was sweet justice! The story of a European race car being driven around Dulaney made instant high school news (largely fostered by me). But it was a true event and I was somewhat of a celebrity because of it. It didn't hurt to add to my mystique as the Parkville kid with great car connections!

Chapter Twenty-One
"BREAKING INTO DULANEY"

My new life in the Valley was solidifying during the year Doug returned home. I was a junior at Dulaney and had settled in to a peculiar, yet livable role. I wasn't a sports guy, being six feet tall and just 130 pounds soaking wet. I didn't like getting sand kicked in my face, so I kept a cool guy persona mixed with enough clown to draw respect from sports and non-sports friends alike. My apparent preppy look and maturity (having older siblings) allowed me easy access to the "in" crowd, but I didn't prefer them. I liked and trusted a select few. I was musical and locally known for it, so that bought me all the self esteem I needed, and, more importantly, a sufficient number of dates! My psychedelic VW added to the playful color of my personality. Having a brother as a race car driver and the car to prove it somehow transmitted an element of daredevil to my own reputation. To be truthful, I enjoyed being a man of mystery. I was a reasonably smart kid, but failed to apply myself and struggled with trigonometry and physics when the college prep track landed me in those classes. I would have rather been playing music, a practical joke, or cruising with "real" friends!

At its core, I was a Parkville guy, and was still holding on to the things that made me who I was. I didn't *want* to become a Dulaneitte, but learned to live in harmony with the natives. I held certain corny notions of right and wrong (except when severely breaking traffic laws), kept friends regardless of their social status, felt compassionate for the little guy or odd ball, and didn't take myself too seriously. In the heady world of "the Valley," those notions were mocked. I pretty much did my own thing. Because Dan Sutphen shared my value system, we were closer than brothers. He was chief among the select few who *really* knew me. Interestingly, he was a star Dulaney football player and was beloved by our entire class. But Dan sought to keep his balance and his individualistic attitude, and I knew the thoughts and feelings that coursed through him were precisely the same as mine!

Dan and I drew much closer during our sophomore year when he discovered he had advanced cancer and might well die. It was a brutal year for him, being one of the very first patients in the United States to be placed in an experimental trial group to use a treatment called "chemotherapy." He would drive to Johns Hopkins to have it administered and often swing by my home afterwards. But the chemo's vicious affects would set in and he'd then head for his own home and bed for days. Not that it mattered (at all), but Dan drove a red 1965 Corvair Monza convertible back and forth. It was one piece of "cool factor" luxury he could enjoy at an otherwise cruel and punishing life juncture. His Monza was the first year of the second generation Corvairs and was considered by many of us to look like mini-Corvettes, but in my mind and his, it would be forever linked with these painful memo- 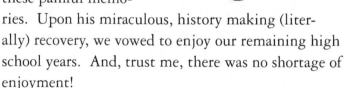 ries. Upon his miraculous, history making (literally) recovery, we vowed to enjoy our remaining high school years. And, trust me, there was no shortage of enjoyment!

As '68 progressed, I found myself smitten by a particular cutie named Peggy. She was a member of the "in" crowd and predictably voted Miss Personality our senior year. By chance, a date materialized out of one of those group things which generated enough face time for me to win charm points to prove I was worthy of a real date. It worked, and one date led to another. I wasn't particularly comfortable in her circles, but she was adorable, and I played the part in order to stay close. This led me to knowing her six closest, good looking and crazy girl friends, including a girl named Fran. Her rather handsome troop would head off to Ocean City, Maryland every summer and effortlessly land jobs "working and flirting" at beach front restaurants. We guys always followed close behind, would unearth their annual beach communes, and crash for days at a time. All of our hotrod activities would also migrate to O.C., and cruising became a parade-like activity where fabulous cars were the stars. The Beach Boys (Catch a Wave), Jan and Dean (Surf City), and The Safaris (Wipe Out) were born from such intoxicating memories. Does anyone wonder why?

This is where I met Fran's boyfriend, Jeff. Jeff was one of the "cooler guys" from the class ahead of us. He drove a pristinely kept "Marimba Red" 1964 Tri-power GTO, four speed with black interior. His upper class status and gold social circle creds weren't the same as mine, but his taste in cars were and we connected on this common ground. Jeff and I found ourselves together frequently as Peggy and  Fran were regularly joined at the hip. So, Jeff being a trusting guy, and with my reputation for handling cars, his GTO kind of became my GTO in so much as he'd let me drive it or take it whenever he was "physically engaged or impaired" (which were pretty often and I need not say more).

And it ran good, *real* good! My first experience with unleashing three deuces on a big block came under Jeff's supervision. I was driving it near our high school, where he lived. The roads were ridiculously wide and straight, providing an open invitation to every car freak to "get on it!" Jeff had this, shall we say, over exaggerated sense of shifter and clutch care. He prided himself in being able to shift so smoothly, matching revs with shifts that it would feel like an automatic trans. He also lifted his foot off the clutch peddle between all shifts and insisted I do the same, particularly when driving his "Goat." The lesson stuck and I still do that today. But as Dr. Jeckle was also Mr. Hyde, all transmission and clutch care went out the window when he would decide to trounce on it. His power shifts were gorilla like slaps, and you had to wonder how he could turn so aggressive after just being so painstaking and fastidious during his "gentle" shifts. Now that's funny!

So with Jeff as passenger, he said to me: "Jump on it as hard as you can!" "As hard as I can?" "Yeah, go ahead. Let me show ya what's she'll do!" And so I did. GTOs, like our Cultess, were intermediate cars called Tempests, and in 1963 the largest engine you could get was a 326 cubic inch V-8. GM had banned its brand from all racing, but a brash designer named John De lorean came up with the idea to stuff a big block in this little car as an "option," getting around the GM rule that nothing bigger than 330 cubic inch engines could be put in A-body cars. While De Lorean thought it would capture the young buyer, Russell Gee worked out the engineering and geometry. The first year's production was set at 5,000 cars, fearing its failure. They had to make over 32,000 in '64 to keep up with demand. The rest is history.

When my right foot crushed the accelerator, the GTO's three twos opened nearly simultaneously. I've had maybe hundreds of four barrels open, but the sound of six barrels opening was exhilarating. The 3,500 pound, 348 horse, 3.90 rear, posi "Tempest" came alive and sprang to red-line. Under pressure to make a "pro" shift, I powered the standard equipment Hurst back into second with an ever so tiny over rev, and gaining confidence pulled off two more shifts of equal quality. We were running right at 110 miles per hour when I backed off. I blew a loud sustained whistle from my lips and cocked my head in his direction. He was beaming at me! Sing along with me, "Little GTO, you know your lookin fine. Three deuces and four speed and a 389..."

Dulaney had its snob factor, yes indeed, but it was Mecca for the car guy. You could stand in the school's parking lot and behold a sea of classic muscle cars that today would be worth millions! And just to mention a few others, Dan and I had a buddy named Ted who lived on one of the huge dairy farms a mile from Dan's house. To our shock, his Dad bought him a new '67 green Malibu Super Sport 396-325 horse hardtop with white interior. Ted never, ever raced that car...EVER! And our friend Bart bought Jeff's identical twin GTO, but it was a '66. Another class-

mate, Glenn, had this way cool '57 Chevy painted
Nausa Blue with a built 327 under the hood. There
was Terry's '68 red Super Sport 350 four speed convertible and Tommy's '67 Falcon Sprint, two door
hardtop, 289 four speed. And because there were
too many others to mention or remember, my final
favorite fantasy car resided directly across the street
from Dulaney. Mike, another classmate, lived in a
white house adjacent to the parking lot entrance (a la
Willoughby Road) and his Dad, a doctor, owned *the*
cleanest, most beautiful 327-300, four speed 1967
Corvette coupe I'd ever laid eyes on. It was Trophy
Blue with matching interior, factory air, headrests,
factory tinted windows, beauty rings and centers,
with slender ring whitewall tires. And it just sat on
the street, day after day, taunting me with its under-
stated beauty.

I was obviously bred, indoctrinated, and incul-
cated to appreciate the automobile, and the person
I had become fed on the love of cars just like this.
They were everywhere. The rebel/artist was brought
alive in me by these fabulous ground-pounding
machines. No matter what I was feeling; which girl
had jilted me, what argument I'd lost, what test I had
flunked, these mechanical creations could revive my
spirit. They could cheat time and space with their
speed, sound, torque, and good looks. Simply put, I
was loony toon for cars!

Chapter Twenty-Two
HERE COME THE PONIES

Let's drop back to May 1965. Cheryl had just graduated from Parkville High. Mom and Dad had decided NOT to traumatize the queen and had allowed her to finish out her senior year there. She commuted daily in the big red (now pink) Olds. She was pretty washed up (the car, not my sister), and Dad went on the prowl for the next family hauler. His fetish for T-Birds was never satisfied, but those had grown bloated and unbabybird-like by '65 and he'd lost interest. Since Uncle Jimmy had bought his Mustang, Dad's affections had turned to this newest Blue Oval offering. He kept threatening to buy one and we kids kept blowing him off with, "Yea, right, Dad. You? Buy a Mustang?"

Mustangs had swooped in and captured the imagination of the entire automotive world. Designed by Lee Iacocca, it was introduced in March 1964 as the 1965 model year car at a base price of $2,371! Over a million were produced in the first eighteen months

(681,551 for '65 and 607,568 for '66). Ford was so caught off guard by its success that some cars left the assembly line with back-up light options as unfilled and unwired "holes." And the 289 front fender engine badge was to denote that option but didn't make it onto a number of cars. With decisions to switch from a generator to an alternator and improve the six cylinder option from the Ford Falcon 170/101 horse to the 200/120 horse six, Ford decided to re-classify the first 121,538 as 1964 ½ model cars. There are still 1964 Mustangs with "Falcon" emblems on the steering wheels.

With the gauntlet laid down, Dad promptly brought home a NEW 1966 maroon Mustang "fastback" (only 27,809 of these made), black interior, automatic (no air, of course), 289 "C" code (2 barrel). With the fastback option adding $191 to the base price, we were impressed that Dad had actually bought an additional feature on a new car, and we were thrilled with the  overall decision. Admittedly, we felt a bit guilty that our goading so easily produced the correct results. We all piled in to take a ride. As Cheryl and I crawled to our places on the rear seat, we thought the back bench was so hip looking, this curved, modern looking slab contoured to the floor, with a half inch of foam covered in pleated vinyl. It even folded down to give the fastback a very-mini station wagon storage platform. The front seats were buckets and that in itself denoted a "cool" factor since bucket seats were still identified with sports cars. Mom was half excited, half dubious that such a small car would serve the family needs.

As usual, she was right. We took our first trip to Rochester, New York to see my brother, which was a six-hour ride in one direction. By the time we had reached Doug's, sis and I were grossly complaining about that "hip" back seat! The thing was SO uncomfortable and there was no position one could contort to make it otherwise. "Hip" more accurately meant "hip displacement!" Then, while driving home, we encountered a snow storm and the Mustang proved no match for icy roads. The dual issues of Cheryl and I giving the parents a fit and sliding half way back to Baltimore made this the trip from hell! Okay, so the "fastback" wasn't a good family car decision. Dad gallantly put up a good fight and we all commented on the car's other virtues since we were complicit in its purchase, but that back seat was murder, and it eventually killed Dad's dreams of keeping his little Mustang.

Speaking of dying, the old VW finally croaked in mid 1968, right around Doug's return home (You might actually say I dealt the bug a death blow!) She wasn't worth trying to salvage, and I was both happy and sad over her demise; happy since now I could shop in earnest for a cooler car, sad since we had been through a lot together. I was a junior in high school and working part-time at Greater Baltimore Medical Center where my sister worked. I also was doing the music thing, playing drums and picking up gigs on Saturday nights. I was making some decent side money, and I was ready to go shopping!

Dad had traded his Mustang just five months after its purchase and returned to a trusted make Mom was sure to like, a 1966 Delta 88 Oldsmobile. You had to appreciate that he was buying an Olds in the same year it was produced. Dad had now bought two new cars in a row!! He had almost come full circle, but we still couldn't get the man to *really* option out a car. He remained hopeless in that regard! So here was this two door dark grey hardtop Olds with an AM radio and no air conditioning. It had black vinyl interior and with the Baltimore summers punishingly hot, we insisted that he at least add AC. Dad succumbed and went off to Montgomery Ward to have a cheap aftermarket unit installed. It was one of those boxes that looked like a restroom hand dryer hanging beneath the dash. The appendage was so inefficient that you had to have your face six inches from the grates to feel cool air.

We drove that Olds to California one summer, and Dad was determined to prove that his air conditioner choice was a good one. Cheryl was unable to go (I think she was the smart one), so I had invited a neighbor friend to join us. We were somewhere in the Arizona desert late in the afternoon, and I remem-

ber the interior temperature rivaling the outside
temperature. We had been in the car for four days
and had learned that the morning AC efficiency was
reasonably comfortable, but by 2 p.m. we'd start to
wilt. That tiny air conditioner would be cranked to
"Max," and Mom and Dad would be suffering in the
mid-80s, while the backseaters were roasting at 100
plus degrees! The back and forth sounded like this:
"Dad, we're dying back here!" "It's not that bad!"
"You come back here and see!" "I can't. I'm driving!"
"Let's just open the windows!" "Can't. What do ya
think we bought an air conditioner for?" We made it
through the trip, but oh how I cursed Montgomery
Ward!

With the VW expiration, Dad was forced to
purchase the next used "house" car, and it was another
Olds. Man, we were on an Olds roll! I was less willing to "commandeer" this one as my own, knowing it
would impede progress towards my next dream ride.
I had to admit, though, it was a pretty nifty sled.
She was a white four-door 1963 F-85 Oldsmobile
and, get this, she had "factory air!" These cars were
introduced in '61 as "senior" compacts or "intermedi-
ates" built on the GM 112 inch unibody frame. As a
cousin of the Buick Special and Pontiac Tempest, it
was equipped with GM's itsy-bitsy 215 Cubic inch
V-8, which churned out 155 horses in two barrel
dress and 185 with a four. There was a Jetfire addition which sported a Garett TO-3 turbo in '62 and
'63 and produced one horse per cubes, 215. These

were the forerunners to the soon-to-be-very-cool 442 and its more famous cousin, the GTO. But ours was the sedan version with a two barrel carb. It wasn't a bad little machine, and I think Dad was hoping I'd adopt it. Granted, it was a perfect date car, having a bench front seat. I could quickly tell how my date was going. If she was plastered against the door, it would be a short night. And the opposite, well, let's just say I'm glad we had air conditioning! We should have taken *it* to California!

Between earning some side dough, my friends' newer rides, and my brother's continuing influence, I felt the calling for a "four speed steed!" Dad would be a big part of the financing, so his approval would be crucial, and since my drag racing fiasco, I had endeavored to at least look the part of Mr. Responsible. He and Mom had somewhat re-warmed to my charming ways! So, with a dollar figure in mind, I went car shopping. It wasn't long before I discovered a low mileage midnight blue 289 Mustang coupe with white and light blue "pony" interior and a four speed. We'd already had a fling with a Pony and would have liked to have kept it, had it not been crippling for the children. I quickly deduced that I could bring one back into the family under the ownership it was correctly destined... young, great looking guys like me! With the test drive a suc-cess, I dragged Dad back with me to seal

the deal. He even agreed to help with the payments
(he really liked *his* Mustang!). I had nabbed myself
a "Stang!" Rated at 225 horses with a four barrel in "A" code dress, it was a respectable performer.
This one had the optional pony interior, wood grain
accents, and extra nice seat coverings. Mine did not
have the "Ralley Pack" tach - clock combo, but I'd
later remedy that with a fashionable Sun tach, which
I stylishly perched on the column. Even the back seat
was more livable!

I was ecstatic, owning my own Mustang. Its V-8
had a sweet low Ford rumble and she ran with the
bigger ponies, albeit on their heels. I did discover
early on that it wasn't a Corvette killer after having
my doors blown off in several street altercations. One
in particular was quite memorable and embarrassing.
I had rolled up to a light on Perring Parkway, a four
lane wide thoroughfare a few miles from the house.
It was nighttime and a stock 1965 Vette coupe nosed
up next to me on my left. Corvettes in '65 ran a
range of 327s from 250 horses up to 300, 350, 365
and 375 horsepower, and without the noted 396 or
427 "blister" or "stinger" on the later model hoods,
I couldn't tell if I was gonna drag a 250 h.p. version
or a 365 monster. But I was going to race a Corvette,
and it wouldn't take long to find out its degree of
meanness. We both revved simultaneously. I held at
about 3,500 r.p.m.s the instant before green (which
produced my best launches). The light changed and I
dumped the clutch. Between wheel spin and traction

he totally jumped me by a half a car and I knew that there were more than 250 horses residing under his hood. We both grabbed second and the Vette simply walked away. By third gear, he had four cars on me. Geezz, I was not just beat, but pulverized! Then, to add insult to injury, I had to pull next to him again at the following light. I good naturally looked over and shrugged my shoulders, and he just laughed and we both eased away knowing there would be no rematch.

I determined I would either have to bolt on a bigger four barrel married to a cam, and hang headers to play that game again, or simply go buy a Vette. But in the meantime, I had decided to keep her pretty stock, money being what it was, and I added small touches as I could afford them. These included removing the pony from the grill and adding a small Mustang badge to its right side, a la 350 G.T.s. I put glass packs and the "in style" hood locks, and traded out the hubcaps for mags. I slightly jacked the rear suspension and ditched the whitewalls in favor of the largest blackwalls I could find. Within six months, the little Mustang ran smartly and at least looked like a runner. I'd hang on to her for my senior year in high school and into my first year of college. It then it made its way into Jimmy Gochenour's garage for another six years.

Before I leave the Mustang memories, there were three more Mustangs that deserve honorable mention. One of my close high school buds, Alex, bought a new Mach I in 1969. It was a green 351, 290 horse-

power, four barrel (Cleveland motor) with an optional
three speed tranny. (It was on the lot that way! Most
of the three speed Mach I's were the two barrel Wind-
sor motor producing 250 horses). One could order
Mach Is with two different 351s, a 390/320 horse (S
code) and two 428s, the CobraJet (Q code) and the
Super CobraJet (R code).

Tommy, Doug's friend, had a four speed Super
CobraJet with the shaker hood (standard on the 428s),
and he drove it with pure malice. Believe it or not,
this guy was a Maryland State Trooper whose motivation for his profession had more to do with legally
speeding and less to do with law enforcement. He
found himself pulled over more than initiating the
pulling! He and my brother were running at about
130 m.p.h. one night and passed another trooper sitting under an overpass. Doug recalled Tom quickly
reciting the trooper's car number out loud and joked
that he knew this one well! He let his comrade catch
up, pull him over, and do the walk up thing to his
window. Doug said the conversation went something
like this: State Trooper: "Tommy, not you again!"
Tommy: "Yep, Jack, it's me." State Trooper: "Well,
Tom, this is gonna have to stop!" Tommy: "Come on,
Jack, where's your sense of humor!"

And then there was Hazo! Hastings Merryman
dated one of Peggy's friends from the six-pack of
girls mentioned earlier. He was a year ahead of us
in school, so we didn't get a lot of face time. But I
did hitch a ride one time in his brand new, factory

ordered "Raven Black" 1969 Mustang Boss 429 with
a 429/375 horse (Z code) engine (which later dynoed
at somewhere over 460 horsepower) and a 4 speed
transmission. There
were 858 '69s and 499
'70s made to meet the
NASCAR homolo-
gation target of 500. Its engine, the "semi-hemi,"
produced 460 foot pounds of torque. By 1969, I had
ridden or driven several Boss 302s and their evil twin,
Z-28s. They were high winding, kick in the pants
kind of cars, but this was a lethal weapon and I knew
when I climbed in that it would scare the pajub-
bies out of me. But I had trained on one particularly
nasty Corvette (yet to be disclosed) as well as Walley's
Cougar and was somewhat ready for whatever the
machine could dish out. We drove onto Pot Springs
Road and Hazo lined up mid-road for our launch,
something I had been doing now for years. It was
kind of a rolling start, but when he dropped the ham-
mer, the engine came on like a freight train, and the
beast simply didn't hook up until three or four seconds into second gear! The G force was astounding,
an amazing display of brute strength and torque. As
stupid quick as it was, Walley's 390 big block (with
help from his father's gang) was almost as bad. I was
not completely overwhelmed as a novice might be. I
even wondered if old Wall or brother Doug's latest
wheels (the next chapter) could take on this monster.

Honestly, such creations so over matched their tire and drive train combinations, we couldn't know their full potential unless they were unleashed on the quarter mile track with slicks. Today, half the horsepower can outperform their best street numbers. But had I known at the time that this car and the one Forrest Green ZL-1 $7,500 Camero I saw at Fox Chevrolet would become two of the most treasured vehicles on earth, I'd have paid more attention (since that would have been the only thing I could afford to pay!). Who would have ever guessed?

Chapter Twenty-Three
AND THEN THERE WERE OUR CORVETTES!

My most vivid memories of car nirvana occurred in 1969, my senior year at Dulaney. It was a turbulent time in history, and my class represented the epicenter of change and cultural rebellion. Cute songs and innocent television were giving way to deeper and darker sounds and themes. The Beatles, Jimi Hendrix, Led Zeppelin, and Cream were nearing their zeniths, exploring mind expansion and delivering albums like *Abbey Road* and *Good Bye*, and songs such as "Come Together!" The group Chicago burst on the scene with their debut album "Chicago Transit Authority."

All around me, things were verging on chaos. The Vietnam War had escalated and 543,000 troops were on the ground. Thirty-three thousand had already been killed. Our first "known" casualty, Jerry, from the previous graduating class, had lost both legs thanks to a land mine. Acid rock, love-ins, and peace signs pushed the movement to the extreme. My preppy appearance morphed even further into the new "Mod" look, with long sideburns and hair that covered my ears and collar. Gone were the khakis and penny loafers, replaced with radical bell bottoms and platform shoes. The Woodstock Festival was held at a farm in Bethel, New York and attracted 350,000 that summer, but my buddies and I didn't go simply because we were heading to upper West New York later that October for the Grand Prix at Watkins Glen, and event equally wild in reputation!

Easy Rider hit the movies, and Hurricane Camille hit the Mississippi coast killing 248. The Who introduced a rock opera called "Tommy" while the National Guard was being pelted with rocks in race, gay and war riots throughout the country. While the Beach Boys were trying to get out of bed with Capital Records, John Lennon got in bed with Yoko Ono. Armstrong and Aldrin walked on the moon while the Manson cult walked into a living room and murdered five. And the U.S. military instituted the draft lottery, guaranteeing enough replacement young men to fight the "Conflict" in Vietnam. The lottery numbers corresponded to each day in the year, and ones birthday became forever linked to a number drawn randomly from a hat. Numbers one to one hundred and fifty, out of a possible three hundred and sixty-five, were almost virtually assured of being drafted. My number was eight!

Yes, it was a crazy time and each of us sought to cope, medicate or escape, whether it be with drugs or drink, hard rock or hard fun, fast girls or fast cars. Of course, there was the group of "steady Eddies" who studied and missed the revolution all together. But the majority of us were swept up in its current. I chose several routes of coping, much to the alarm and concern of my parents. But I wasn't alone. With our nation's elders deciding which young men should die for a cause no one could agree upon, the theme became "Let us eat, drink, and be merry, for tomorrow we may die!" My hair and clothes concealed a patriot. I was from a long line of brave veterans, and prepared to fight, but even I couldn't see the logic any longer.

Meanwhile, the big three auto makers played right into our generation's hands. It's as if they heard each of us say, "Build me a get-away car...make it fast and make it cool! Life is short, and I need to make a lasting impression!" One radical car after another came off the assembly line. Rat-powered Novas and Hemi-powered Cudas, big block Vettes and snake-powered Fords, they were all just another expression of rebellion. If a guy needed a land rocket to take his mind off of an embattled culture, he could order one up.

In 1968, Brother Doug purchased a 260 V-8 Falcon Sprint Convertible as his first stateside car. It was a 1964, four speed car and really very cool, but

under powered and not to his liking. So, he traded
it for what would become one of the fastest cars he
or I would ever pilot. I'm not sure Doug was fully
apprised of all of the mechanical alterations made to
his 1965 code "GG" (Glen Green) Corvette convertible, but whatever had been done was amazingly
effective. It had started life as one of the 771 fuel
injection (FI) Corvettes made that year. Its previous
owner had scrapped the injection system in favor of a
conspicuous high rise manifold and a 780 duel-feed
Holley carb, and then found it necessary to put on a
1967 427 stinger hood to accommodate the tower-
ing intake system. After some apparent cam work
and other never discovered goodies, the otherwise
stock looking Vette re-emerged on the streets with
unknown gobs of horsepower, surely well north of
400. With an upgraded, neck-snapping, gas-guzzling
4:11 posit-traction rear end and a short "snick-snick"
M21 close-ratio Muncie transmission, this Corvette
was a certified street dragster. In 1965, Corvette
offered four high revving 327 engines. But right out
of the box, the 365 and 375 horse versions had solid
lifters, larger valves and 11:1 compression. The tires
were anemic 8.75 by 14s off the showroom, but Doug
found the largest tires you could stuff in the wheel

wells, G60 14s, and
wedged them on the
back of the car. It
would need every
inch of rubber. Let

me repeat myself....I had never driven or ridden in any production vehicles as quick, including Walley's screamer and Hazo's 429 Boss. Even though it was only a small block, it could yank the left front wheel off the ground in two gears, and until you've driven a semi-wheel standing car, you've not driven a fast hotrod! It was one bad-to-the-bone mother!

Doug's car was clad in black interior and a black convertible top. He later purchased a black vinyl hardtop, which in itself led to a hilarious episode. He had found the top in the paper and visited the seller, who had the otherwise hard to find accessory in his garage. Doug thought it was in reasonably good condition, and paid the man $300. He and a friend put it on the car and drove back to the house. Later that night, Doug was partying hard at the newly formed Omega Sigma Phi non-school, semi-adult frat house. This "social experiment" had been thrown together by a group of his twenty something friends, mostly as a place to hang out, party, and crash! Trust me; there was no school within thirty miles of the place. My parents hated the idea of this alternative pad, not so much for Doug but for its influence on me, who'd visit the old three-story residence quite frequently. My then musical group, the "Superband," would play there as a standing Friday night gig. We'd make $125 plus all of the hydration we wanted. And the girls were not bad either! See why my parents hated it? But the parties were legendary and if traced backwards, one would probably find it the motivation for the hit movie "Animal House!"

It was around midnight and Doug and a buddy decided to stretch the Vette's legs on 695 (the Balti-more Beltway). They were doing somewhere in the neighborhood of 130 m.p.h, when they were spot-ted and pulled over by a veteran state trooper and three trooper "training" cadets. Doug described it as a "teachable moment" for the new recruits! When told what he was clocked at and then asked what in the world possessed him to be driving that fast, Doug replied, with a straight face, "I just bought this top and wanted to test it at high speed!" It wasn't his lame excuse that kept him out of jail. It was his trooper pal, Tommy, who also happened to be a frat brother, and Doug's passenger that night!

Back to the car, it was to become my first Corvette "driving" experience. And what a way to break me in. Whew! If you haven't had the pleasure of sit-ting behind the wheel of a C-2 (1963-67) Corvette,

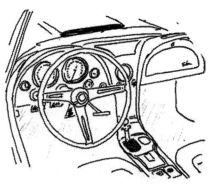

you must find a way to do so. All great cars should give the driver the impression of riding between the tires rather than over them. The "hood" view from the driver seat in these older Vettes was exactly that. To my left and right were the muscular fender bulges (as if riding on the back of a real Stingray!). In this case, the "stinger" hood rose to add a menacing third dimension of contour, so the driver was looking down a valley on the left side of the hood. Recalling the '63 Z06 experience, you sat low and comfortable, greeted with a business-like instrument cluster arrayed around a huge faced tach and speedometer, nestled inside an arching dash, a design que which still lives today. Its optional wood grain steering wheel, although anorexic in comparison to today's wheels, was the height of "cool" and gave one the impression of steering a quality sports car.

I turned the key over and brought the small block to life, an engine note I still remember to this day. I recall the car wouldn't run on any fuel other than Super Shell or 260 Sunoco... period. If you tried to sneak a cheaper grade into the tank, it would choke and miss as if the timing was off ten degrees. But my goodness, what a difference when the right gas was in the tank. And the M21 was a joy to shift, its throws short and precise, and nearly impossible to screw up. Leaving in first gear was a cinch because leaving in fourth gear was too. The 4:11 rear made the Vette plenty alive and trackable in every gear. We could actually smoke the tires leaving in third, not to mention burning down an entire rear set when leaving hard in first.

Doug rode with me on my maiden voyage, and I quickly determined I was way over my head and that

this Vette deserved colossal respect. In fact, after he
and I drove the car for a year, we never reached its
potential. It was always way quicker, way meaner than
our courage would allow. I brought it up through
the gears and started getting a feel for its clutch and
handling. I had it for ten or fifteen minutes before I
got on it halfway through second and just into third.
It was so shocking that I backed off instantly and had
to regain my composure. I knew then, this car would
either significantly raise my driving skills or simply
kill me. Thankfully, it stayed in the hands of a race
car driver far more skilled than me.

Weeks went by and Doug became more and more
generous with the keys. The first time he let me
drive it to school, I nearly fainted from excitement. I
actually had trouble sleeping the night before, knowing I would be parking a Glen Green Corvette in my
school lot. Of course, I took great care in driving it
to school. Word spread quickly that my brother's car
was in the parking lot, with its and his reputation
preceding the visit. That afternoon, I grudgingly volunteered (yeah, right) to take a buddy for a short ride
just to further cement the car's creds.

Chip was my first victim and although I normally
turned left out of the parking lot and drove past
Miginky's '67 Vette, I turned right and headed up
to the straightaway where I had abused Jeff's GTO.
Turning left onto his road, I nailed the accelerator at
about 2,500 r.p.m.s. The front left torque up (not off
the ground) and the back end broke traction, tell-

ing me that I needed to lift to half throttle or risk an uncontrolled run or a blown "something"! I didn't want to return the car to Doug on a wrecker, that's for sure. But we went up through the gears with enough pulling and G's to get Chip to start swearing. Loudly! I recall rolling back up to the school and having him, not me, jump out and start gossiping about its fantastic power.

I'm sure I'm not aware of the many escapades my brother experienced while driving the Corvette, but I have one final memory of this particular car's glory. You may recall the Porsche 356 story and our trip through the twistees of Loch Raven. Interspaced in that winding road were several one mile straightaways, and on Sunday afternoons, one of these stretches became a "cruise in" for some of Baltimore's hottest rides. From Hemi Cudas to street rods, each side of the road was lined with both luscious lookers and, some day, million dollar cars. Although burnouts were a later era phenom, you were encouraged to stage in the center of the street, pull a hole shot and run hard through the gears, as the entertainment for these gatherings! Fortunately, the road was wide but never the less the activity was highly illegal and being so, it seemed to foster an escalating one-upsmanship as the weeks went by. Each Sunday became more and more of a show, and the reputation of Loch Raven spread throughout the city.

Doug and I visited the last Sunday this event would ever occur. With the Corvette loping and all eyes on us, Doug centered the car, revved to five grand and side-stepped the clutch. The Vette lurched sideways and the rear tires went up in smoke. But as it pulled into traction, the left wheel broke contact with the ground and came back down slowly until second gear. I recall everyone pointing and hands shooting up to cover their mouths, or squeezing the side of the face in astonishment. Others threw their fists in the air in jubilant excitement as Doug pulled it hard into second and repeated the wheel off stunt. It was a ridiculous display of power and as we broke off the run and circled back, spectators on each side of the road were clapping and cheering for the Glen Green Vette. The next Sunday, Baltimore County Police were positioned up and down that street, daring anyone to park. Within several weeks, "No Parking" signs were posted every fifty feet, lining the now quiet straightaway. Darn those pesky cops! Our fun was over, but having the last laugh and the memories, was forever rich!

A footnote to Lock Raven...Doug's friend Charlie bought a white 1969 Corvette with red interior and the very rare L-88 427 engine option. This car would eventually fetch some of the largest collector dollars in history. He had owned it for one week when it was stolen. The police did not have to look long. Its body and chassis only were recovered from the Lock Raven reservoir. It had been professionally stripped - engine, trans, gauges, wheels and tires and then sunk in a section of the reservoir where when the water

receded, there she lay. It was a sad, sad day for Charlie.
But not that sad....with the insurance money, he
promptly bought a blue tri-power 427. Within two
weeks he went air born at high speed, landed and
ripped the oil pan off, crushing the crank, destroying
the engine. He had no insurance this time around.
Charlie, Charlie, Charlie!!

Doug kept his '65 for several years, long enough
to influence me to buy my own. Since I was more the
artist than the rebel, I wasn't interested as much in
the crazy horsepower (I'd had all of that I could stand)
as I was in that clean look of the Miginsky's Trophy
Blue Vette. Their coupe was the high water mark in
my opinion, representing power, beauty and class! So
in 1970, with enough money in hand to buy a several
year older one, I started shopping. Within weeks I
found a 1966 "Trophy Blue" convertible, 327/300,
with a close ration four speed! It had a white top and
black interior, low mileage and the seller took my
offer with very little hassle. In '66, the Corvettes were
hardly indistinguishable from the '65s. The coupe
had done away with
the side roof vents,
and the rocker panel
strip and the grill
were altered ever so
slightly. Mechanically,
the 1966 only offered two small block horsepower
versions, 300 and 350, and the 396/425 horse in
the 1965 gave way to the 427 with two horsepower

options, 390 and 425 b.h.p. Although the 396 and 427 sported the same horsepower, the 427 produced 460 foot pounds of torque versus 415 for the lesser 396. Mine had the not so glamorous stock hubcaps, so I quickly remedied that by buying 1967 silver vented wheels, beauty rings and centers, giving my car a fraternal twin appearance to the Mininsky coupe.

Every now and then, Detroit would produce a factory car whose performance would defy all explanation. We muscle car guys knew what to expect from the average 327 Chevy or the 351 Ford, but there was this anomaly that would occur on the production line, where the engine parts fit together perfectly, constituting essentially a factory blue printed engine. My little 300 horse Vette ran exceptionally well. I can't say it was one of those anomalies, but it never failed to tach up effortlessly when called upon, and, of course, I called upon it frequently. I was leaving a night club one evening after our band had performed and rolled up in the slow lane next to a 383 Plymouth Roadrunner. These things were everywhere because they were cheap and fast muscle, built around a motor and these radically long Hurst Pistol grip shifters. At 335 horse stock, it was a formidable contender. And if you tangled with the 440/390 six pack, you could expect to get spanked. For $715 one could upgrade these Roadrunners to a 425 horse Hemi, and you better have brought your biggest gun to duel with this, the baddest of the bad boys. We all left Hemis alone!

It was late, and I was more interested in getting to bed than drag racing a clearly designated 383 "meep meep!" However, he insisted by using his index finger to point down the road, to which I replied with a finger point as well. We tached, the light changed and I simply blew his doors off through three gears. I then shut it down and turned right using my blinker, which he had adequate time to see. He was humiliated, I'm sure, and I had the satisfaction of a clean kill with a very predicable weapon. It was my sweet revenge for that very bad Corvette thrashing I took in my Mustang! What goes around comes around, right?

Three other memories with this Vette...late one evening, I was entering the Baltimore Beltway at the Charles Street entrance, a long, downhill ramp that simply invited a hard acceleration. I tached to five grand in first gear, and quick shifted into second, when to my great dismay, the clutch pedal arm broke cleanly in two! Yes, the forged metal arm broke!! I remember sensing the tension in my left foot giving way and it falling helplessly forward to the firewall and this thing hitting my shin. "What the h...?" Using my foot, I felt around in the dark for a pedal, which had apparently vanished. I reached down with my left hand, feeling for anything, and came up with a clutch arm and pedal in my hand. "Great!!" Here, I was stuck in second gear. I tossed the pedal into the passenger seat and began to quickly process my next moves. I had exited the ramp and was riding on the Beltway shoulder at about 25 m.p.h. I realized I was an eighth of a mile from the next exit ramp. If I made it to the top of that ramp I would have to either shut it down or run the light. But to stay on the Beltway might relegate me to the "He may never return!" MTA status of Kingston Trio fame. This was way pre-cell phone days, and my only option was to nurse this thing back to somewhere close to the house.

So I took the exit, nursed it up to the traffic light, where, by God's grace, there was no traffic and simply eased onto Charles Street. I traveled a block to the next light and, again, as if the Red Sea had parted, I was able to make this smooth, wide U-turn and head back to the opposite Beltway cloverleaf to direct me back to the house. It was miraculous! I swung down around the entrance ramp onto 695 and headed home, all the while traveling at about 25 m.p.h.! I mean, it was a great gear to get stuck in. I could have upshifted to third with little effort, but instead decided as I neared the off ramp to downshift to first (hold your ears!), and creep onto my road to home. From there I encountered two lights where I was forced to shut it down. If you've ever started a car in gear you'll know my restarts were of the bucking bronc variety. I then made it two miles back to my house. The next day I had more than one mechanic on the phone say, "Your clutch pedal did what??"

I owned my Vette for three years. Brother Doug had remarried and was living on the west side of

Baltimore, not far from the famed "frat House." I'd visit him and his new wife regularly, and frequently crash at their place rather than make the trek back over to my house. Doug had just purchased an "Elkhart Green Metallic" (code 946) 1972 Corvette with saddle interior, a 350/255 horse, and an automatic trans. It was pretty weak considering our history. He could only chose from 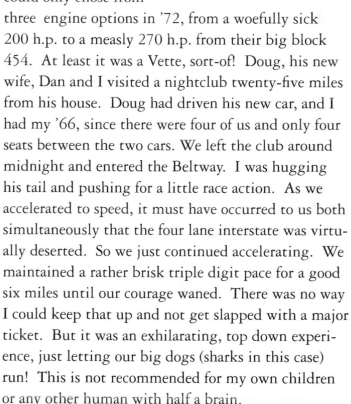 three engine options in '72, from a woefully sick 200 h.p. to a measly 270 h.p. from their big block 454. At least it was a Vette, sort-of! Doug, his new wife, Dan and I visited a nightclub twenty-five miles from his house. Doug had driven his new car, and I had my '66, since there were four of us and only four seats between the two cars. We left the club around midnight and entered the Beltway. I was hugging his tail and pushing for a little race action. As we accelerated to speed, it must have occurred to us both simultaneously that the four lane interstate was virtually deserted. So we just continued accelerating. We maintained a rather brisk triple digit pace for a good six miles until our courage waned. There was no way I could keep that up and not get slapped with a major ticket. But it was an exhilarating, top down experience, just letting our big dogs (sharks in this case) run! This is not recommended for my own children or any other human with half a brain.

Oh, yes, and the night I drag raced the Roadrunner ...my Vette was filled with my beautiful and hard earned set of woodgrain "Rogers" drums. Did you know you could get an entire drum set inside a Corvette? My passenger seat accommodated the base drum, a snare and tom-tom were on the passenger floor; high hat and cymbal stands were in the well behind me, and cymbals were wedged between the door and the base. Our band's base player, Dennis, owned the "band" van in which we hauled our gear, but every now and then something would go haywire or plans would change, and we'd have to haul our own stuff. If you ever need to pack out a Corvette, call me. I'm an expert!

Finally, I have the fondest memories of Dan and me driving my Vette to Ocean City, top down, on a warm summer day. "What a Beautiful Morning" by the Rascals came on the radio, and it became one of those moments...two best buddies, not a care in the world, heading to a beach paradise in a totally cool car. To this day I crank up the radio whenever that song comes on!

Chapter Twenty-Four
"LET IT BE!"

And so I crammed ten years worth of life into the "five year plan." It left me with some crazy and colorful memories, born from stretching and shaping encounters. I didn't mature as an academic or an athlete, but I did pile on random life points and lived way faster than most young men, always more for the moment than for the future. By God's grace, it didn't kill me and I do frequently utilize my significantly developed risk tolerances, but I don't recommend letting your teens learn life lessons this way! Not to make excuses, but I was a sensitive kid, hurt by leaving the comforts of Parkville, and I decided to "let it out and let it in" as Paul McCartney phrased it so well. My parents were in a no win situation, feeling they dealt me a mortal social blow, and they probably allowed me more freedoms than most would have. There were plenty of laughs and tears, highs and lows, and forever a testimony in the making. My potential was latent. I knew full well it was there. I just wasn't ready to flip the switch.

With a well developed music and art acumen (my safety nets), a pretty quick wit, a respectable dating life, and a love for fast cars, deeper matters could wait. I wasn't a bum and always carried my weight financially. Although I had been a church going child, my belief system was not very well formed, but I knew what good character looked like and actually exhibited it occasionally. For example, college was just okay, but I insisted on paying for it myself so that I could quit if the mood struck me. See? There was just enough character in that example to demonstrate honoring my parents, and just enough "free spirit" to show my slippery side. And interestingly, I was the guy most people sought for counsel and friendship since I was my own person and gave truthful advice at the risk of running off friends. See, there's another example! But I rarely took my own advice… the slip! Most importantly, if I needed a quick get away, there was a fast set of wheels in the driveway!

As I close this era, I want to mention several other "shaping" memories of encounters with automobiles. A young guy, who I deemed our local "Steve McQueen" owned a modest house with a single car front garage about a half a mile from us on Eastridge Road. He was probably early thirties, and from what I saw, actually looked like McQueen. He was rugged looking with wiry blond hair, often clad in a white t-shirt and jeans. Although I'd wave to him

when he'd pass the
house, I never met
him. He had a "real"
289 Cobra, white
with blue strips, in his

garage, plus two BSA motorcycles, at least one being
a 650 Hornet with the up-swept pipes. I never failed
to check out his garage upon passing, and his drive-
bys left me with a star-struck reaction. Forty years
later, I remember *that* scene whenever I open my own
garage door! And, had he kept the Cobra, he'd had a
sweet retirement fund!

Also, when I was twenty and wheeling my Vette
around town, I swung into our local Mercury dealership at the sight of a black 1971 Tom Tjaarda
designed De Tomaso Pantera. Having heard about it
and seen pictures, this was my in-person encounter
with this Italian sport car with Ford running gear.
Being that I was in a pristine '66 Vette, I must have
impressed the salesman that I was mature enough
or had enough of Daddy's money to let me take it
on a test ride. He rode shotgun, of course. But the
experience was intoxicating. The 351 Cleveland
engine pumped out 330 h.p. and was planted right
behind my head. The five speed gearbox and gated
shifter was linked to
the famously noisy
ZF transaxle, but the
shifter under my hand
gave the impression of

driving a Ferrari! Although the early cars had water pump problems, their coachwork was fabulous, and they were the closest thing to "exotics" being sold in American dealerships. I was a highly paranoid driver, having glanced at the $11,000 sticker; almost double that of a new Corvette! But, I did stretch her legs in a couple of gears and stored the memory for such a writing as this.

Then there was a frat brother (I use that term loosely) named Dick who owned a 1964, 282 horsepower, three SU carburetors, DB5 Aston Martin. It was identical to James Bond's car from Goldfinger. Dick's was even silver, but with a blue leather interior, not black. Was there a more famous car in 1963? I doubt it. I was never allowed to drive it. Dick was too smart for that. But I had a half dozen meaningful rides in it, and I learned to appreciate the upper British crust motoring scene. Having piloted MGs and Austin Healeys, this was their faster and more luxurious big British brother. I'm sure Dick grew tired of the worn out question: "Where's the ejection seat button?" These gems are hard to come by now-a-days. One of the James Bond cars, used in publicity tours back in '64, sold in 2006 for over $2 million!

And remember Charlie Gott, my brother's insane friend with the two Corvettes that evaporated in as many weeks? He finally converted to driving a 1970 GTX 440 six-pack (Plymouth for some reason called it the six-barrel...Dodge called it the six pack!), which he named (and subsequently had painted in psychedelic letters on the rear fenders), "Warlord"! Charlie was a real piece of work. I remember this Plymouth ran nearly straight pipes which exited in front of the rear wheel and would shake the dead from their graves. It was as quick as it was loud. And here's the icing on the cake…in some sort of symbiotic symbolism, Charlie legally changed his last name to "Rocket Man!" Need I say more?

Finally, a buddy from college, Tim, ordered up a gorgeous 1970 red 442 W-30 package with white stripes and white interior. These Oldsmobiles had mean looking duel hood snorkels and factory hood locks harboring a 455 cubic inch, 370 horse (grossly underrated) engine and sporting 500 foot pounds of monster torque! This was an automatic car, but had that cool Hurst shift lever adorned with a wooden knob. Tim dated an equally gorgeous blond and to my utter delight, I found out she was an identical twin. With a little encouragement to ask out her sister, I did, and we first double dated in this beautiful vehicle. I found the back seat quite comfortable. But as these things go, after three dates, I determined that Tim's sister had twice the personality because mine had none. Cute, but without conversation, it was hard to make headway! Anyway, the 442 was the star in that story!

In between school, music gigs, dates and parties, we journeyed anywhere and everywhere we wanted. We visited the Grand Prix at Watkins Glen five years in a row. I missed the 1971 race, but Doug went with my friends. It was apparently the wildest of all where someone stole a Greyhound bus from a local diner, drove it into the pits, then into a mud bog where the crowds proceeded to burn it to the ground. As I said, the in-field activities were wild, bordering on riots, and I maybe saw one hour of racing in five years. But life was lived without limits during this era. We'd drive halfway across the country on a dare. A buddy of mine, Jeff, and I saved our money and hitch-hiked all over Europe for ten weeks. We hiked over 3,000 miles, staying in hostiles, bed and breakfasts and sympathetic people's homes. It was fabulous!

My parents allowed me to have freedoms other kids didn't enjoy. They'd raised two older siblings, and, worried that I was not happy, let me explore, experiment, and discover. I happily turned the keys, pulled the shifters, and ran the streets. But there are always consequences. I apparently played right into the hands of Uncle Sam. You can't have that much freedom and stay a full-time college student. I had let my hours slip below the required twelve a semester and when I wasn't a full time college student, the Selective Service came looking for me. And that old lottery number "8" might as well have been number "1"!

PART THREE
"THE REAL WHEELS OF MY LIFE!"

Chapter Twenty-Five
"GIVE ME FIFTY!"

You really can't appreciate how nice it is let your beard grow until a Marine DI's eyeballs are one inch from your throat. He then rises up and moves his mouth to within an inch of your left ear and screams, "YOU MISSED A SPOT SHAVING, SAILOR!!!" And to atone for such a grievous error, you find your-self jogging in fifty pounds of gear for the next hour.

This was (unfortunately) my new life in 1971. In an attempt to avoid being drafted, I quickly resumed my full-time studies at college. I had hoped to alter my new found draft status of 1-A, "Eligible for Military Service," but it wasn't to be. Once you were eligible, like a pit bull, they wouldn't turn loose. I was going to have to put my money where my mouth was. Since my family were Navy men (except my brother...go figure), I wisely scurried to the recruit-ing center. I thought I should choose before I had no choice. Once there, I had a delightful chat with a gentleman who described the virtues of joining a reserve special detachment of Navy personnel called "Seabees"! "You'll love it!" he said with a smile. "AND, if you bring a friend, we'll give you your duty station choice!" Wow, what a nice man, and the Navy sounds so fun! He didn't even mention that little war in Southeast Asia!

I came home and sought out Alex, my Mach 1 Mustang friend, (who also happened to fall into the Selective Service abyss), and I recounted the "virtues" to him. With little hesitation and lots of motivation, we signed up together. Two weeks later, I was "disembarking" (ya like that?) from a Greyhound bus onto a Seabee/Marine base in a muggy, hot, mosquito infested swamp in Mississippi, with a vicious looking drill sergeant barking at each of us as we climbed off the bus. I looked around and in my best Goldie Hawn, said, "Where are the ships and the little white sailor hats?"

In response, I heard, "You're in the Bees, boy! When you join the Navy, you see the world. But in the Bees, son, you dig through it! You got me?" To which I thought, "Uh, great...this is *just* great! I might as well have joined the freakin Marines! Ooh-rah! To my dismay and considerable discomfort, boot camp WAS straight out of the Marine manual. If there were any wishes or complaints, no one gave a flying flip! We were simply trying to stay alive. The military breaks you to rebuild you and there are few as good at that as the Jarheads. Without going into all of the gory details and macho jazz, let's say that's understood and get to how "driving" was related to my stint in the service.

The Seabees were all about building stuff, mostly bridges, air strips, and roads. The standing joke was that we had a life expectancy of six seconds because we had to hit the beach first to clear a path for the Marines. That wasn't exactly true and the Marines weren't amused! But it was true that John Wayne died in only three of his movies. "The Fighting Sea-beas" was one of 'em. When I heard that I said, "This just keeps getting better!!"

Anyway, some guys looked down the "potential vocations" list and picked jobs like surveying or building construction. What, are you kidding me? When I saw "Equipment Operator," I broke my lead checking the box! Within hours I had begun my twenty-six weeks of learning how to drive bull dozers, cranes, graders, semi-tractors, forklifts, and, my favorite, the gigantic earth scraper! Put a bunch of car nut boys behind the wheels of thirty-ton vehicles and you can have some serious fun! What was the Navy thinking?

Having a reasonable amount of college under my belt, they made me a squad leader (like the art of passing on "yelling" had any correlation to education!!). It didn't take long for us to determine that once basic lessons were given and classroom instruction was finished, supervision was spotty. I was supposed to be the supervision, I guess, but these were my boys, my "band of brothers." If we were going to get into equal amounts of trouble, I chose not to lean in management's direction. The military liked its personnel to "learn on the job." We'd be dropped off daily at various air fields and swamps, and after a few minutes of briefing, we would commence beating the living daylights out of U.S. Government equipment. This abuse lasted about nine hours a day. Okay, it was more like two hours, interrupted by drinking coffee and smoking cigarettes for the other seven.

Our first exercise of "building a runway" hadn't even begun when a Deuce and a Half (that's one of those ugly green covered troop hauling trucks) wheeled onto the field lugging a huge, $20,000 diesel powered generator. It was quickly unhooked, its Cummings engine fired off, and one coffee pot was promptly plugged into it! That's it! For weeks, it was the generator for that coffee pot! What's that you're saying about our tax dollars?

And, of course, it didn't take long to identify the crazies and the rebels in the platoon. The Terex TS 14B was a 45 foot- long, twelve-foot high monster piece of equipment with front and rear Detroit engines sandwiching a fourteen cubic yard bed. It was (is) used to plane or "scrape" and carry off large lengths of earth. We practiced on a 300- acre flat dirt field

divided from end to end by a twenty-five foot deep canyon whose sides sloped down to a fifty-foot wide dry river bed. We'd work on either side of the bed, making long scraper runs and then deposit our loads, building hills or "berms," the military term. Then we'd scrape them down and start again. Day in and day out we'd fly around the field growing more confident, easily reaching speeds of fifty on these machines aptly named for their prehistoric look. Thanks to their six speed automatic transmissions, we could palm the steering with one hand in preparation to hold our M16 rifle in the other. We were under strict orders to "never" cross the river bed, but to go around it.

A fellow solider named Mika was fed up with taking the long way around and decided to risk court martial (Captian's Mast in the Navy) by driving "through" the river bed! He attacked it at an angle, flying down one bank, crossing the bed, with the intention of zipping up the other slope, much like state troopers do when they're crossing a median (a scene I had witnessed – or been part of plenty of times!). The military is not big on giving reasons for their rules, but this one was pretty obvious since the dry river bed was not exactly dry. In fact, it was silt, much like quicksand. Surely this Terex is big enough to cross without drama, thought Mika. He made it about halfway, and his giant hulk began to sink, not just up to the wheels but right past the cab, leaving only two feet of exhaust pipe showing... like a periscope! It was a grand show and all of us lined the rim of the canyon, applauding and laughing hysterically. The Navy wasn't laughing as it took four days and two mega cranes to dislodge the Terex from its muddy tomb. We didn't see Mika for a while!

Or there was the time in bulldozer school when we were taught to "slot doze," a procedure in which you drop the blade of your dozer and push dirt forward, then back up and repeat the procedure, making the same slot deeper each time. Our fellow platoon mate, Alfred, kept digging his slot deeper and deeper with each pass. It got to the point where his dozer started disappearing in a hole deeper than the dozer was tall. I recall seeing him backing out; the rear end of the thing going ten feet in the air and then falling to earth like a Sherman tank cresting a steep hill. The last time he drove in, he didn't come out. Picture a chief petty officer staring down in the hole screaming obscenities! We didn't see Alfred for a while either! But what do you expect when the Navy gives a bunch of twenty-year-olds some really cool sandbox toys?

And one of my favorite experiences was tractor-trailer school. For five weeks, we were each assigned our own big rig, which was essentially a deuce-and-a-half with the bed replaced by a fifth wheel (they called them M35 6 x 6s). We were told that the driving test would consist of, among other things, backing tractor and trailer up to a bay door between cones. Once done, we'd be rewarded with a military

CDL driver's license!
By the second week,
most of us had mas-
tered this maneu-
ver, so we filled the
remaining three weeks
with a sport in which

many of us excelled. We would retreat to the most
isolated part of the base, detach the trailer from the
fifth wheel, and free our tractors. Then we posted a
man a quarter of a mile down the base road where he
could declare a winner as we'd drag race these lum-
bering cabs. This went on every waking hours for
three weeks. It was grand fun, racing these ugly old
vehicles, jamming gears and wasting "free" government gas.

But my funniest memory of Navy inefficiency
came at the end of my basic training. A note was
posted in our barracks asking for volunteers to drive
an ambulance during "bivouac." We were about to
engage in serious war games as Vietnam was still hot
and most of us were destined for that fine Asian country. My Dad had been a Navy medic, so I promptly
volunteered for the position, mostly seeing it as an
opportunity to legally drive fast! Of course *that*
was a joke, knowing we'd be driving 4x4 "Cracker
Boxes," as they were called, whose slow speed would
almost assure the patient's death. With my platoon
mate, Chuck, looking over my shoulder expressing
his desire to try it too, I removed the card from the

bulletin board and we reported to the infirmary as instructed in bold letters.

"Hi, I'm Rodger, and this is Chuck, and we're volunteering for ambulance duty!" I said to the petty officer behind the front desk. He took the card from my hand, examined it, gave us both the once over, and said, "Follow me!" We snaked our way through the base infirmary and arrived at a door labeled "Ambulance Drivers." So far, so good! We entered the small room, consisting of only two bunks, a chair, a large wall map and a black telephone. The petty officer said someone would be with us in a moment and to have a seat. We waited ten minutes and in walked another regular sailor, who greeted us with a smile and a handshake. "So, you two are the replacements, huh? Here's the drill...that phone rings (he pointed to the phone) and tells you where the patient or accident is. You look it up on this map, (pointing again) grab a medic (pointing his thumb over his shoulder), report to that location, load the patient, and, depending on the severity, you either run 'em back here or take them off base down to Kessler Air Force hospital ten miles down Ocean Boulevard. Got that?" We stood there stupefied. "Let me take you out to the ambulance, and I'll show you our gear!" he continued.

I can't remember whether it was Chuck or me who mustered the courage to speak, but one of us asked, "You DO know that we've never done this before, don't you?" He kind of grinned and said, "Ya

got to start some-
where. It's a cinch!"
He proceeded to walk
us around this Cadil-
lac ambulance, rat-

tling off details such as, "Here's the siren, and here's
the interior light. There's the radio and if you have
to go off base, radio ahead to the guard house. Here,
let me show ya…" This went on for ten minutes.
By now I'd starting turning white. Holly mother of
Jupiter, I was going to be driving a real ambulance
with zero experience! The only consolation was that I
had Chuck with me, but he was, unfortunately, more
thunderstruck than me. Things on base happened so
often this way, you grew accustomed to it, and it was
useless questioning authority. You just did what you
were told.

We returned to the "Drivers" room and the petty
officer reminded us: "Wait for the phone to ring! If it
does, grab a corpsman on duty and head out!" Then
he said, "Have a good night. Someone will spell you
first thing in the morning!" Off he went. Chuck and
I stood there looking at one another. This is gonna
be bad, I remember thinking. Chuck voiced his grave
concerns (no pun intended), and we agreed that if
that phone rang, I'd be the first driver and he'd be co-
pilot. Chuck volunteered to canvas the infirmary and
identify the corpsman who would surely know the
ropes. Thankfully, he returned in a few minutes, with
the medic in tow. At least this guy seemed

worried that we were a couple of "know nothings." But we launched in, asking a ton of questions and in his growing importance, he forgot that we were dumb and dumber. We pumped him for over an hour and began to feel reasonably assured that we could at least fake this for one night. We chose bunks and began our vigil, neither of us sleeping, both of us staring at that little black telephone willing it not to ring.

Morning arrived, and realized we had dodged a huge bullet. The phone never rang. We were exhausted from the tension and fear. It spilled out in our nervous laughs when a corpsman showed up as promised to put us out of our misery. We high-tailed it back to our platoon and reported to the OOD (Officer of the Day), who sternly barked, "Where have you guys been? You're listed as AWOL!" "What?" I exclaimed. "We were at the infirmary as instructed." I pulled out the bulletin board card and showed him the instructions. He said, "You idiots, you were sup-posed to report to the Bivouac infirmary, not the main base one!" I said, "With all due respect, sir, does it say that on the card?" He looked again, shook his head and said, "That's the Navy for ya!" And if this debacle wasn't enough, our platoon officer insisted that Chuck and I were now the official drivers and instructed us to report to the base licensing office where, without so much as a single question, the clerk happily typed on my military license, "Ambulance Driver!" I have that license to this day as a reminder that brains can always be trumped by authority!

But life in the military ended up being a good thing for Alex and me. We both settled into the various routines, looking every bit the part of a special detachment, uniforms tailored, blocked hats (fatigue cap put on a mold and sprayed with cans of starch... okay, its a military thing!) and boots spit shined to a mirror glaze. We were given the privilege of bringing our cars back to base after basic training, and the hotrodding began in earnest at every furlough. Life resembled normalcy except now we were more disciplined if not more mature; and we had real jobs, thanks to Uncle Sam. Since this was the Navy reserves, I ended up being stationed stateside (a little education goes a long way), enjoying a short active duty as long as I committed to six more years of service. I returned home with a deep gratefulness for a non-Vietnam enlistment and a new determination to tackle whatever was ahead!

Chapter Twenty-Six
"FLORIDA, HERE I COME!"

I milled around the house for a few months just savoring the civilian life. I easily resumed my work at a local hospital where my sister and now terrific brother-in-law, John, were employed. This had been my regular evening gig since I was sixteen, while playing music was my less regular "starving artist" occupation. But my days were open and I was prepared to return to school when a golden opportunity struck.

My buddy Dan had moved to the land of sun and fun, Fort Lauderdale, while I was away. He snagged a job at a beach surf shop, and, while chatting with him by phone, he extolled the many perks of living in Lauderdale, including details of its exotic, two-legged wildlife! Of course, I was urged to join him and thought I should probably take him up on such an offer while unattached and not bridled by school work. Without hinting that I was making plans, I quietly sold my Vette (I recall I had two buyers

standing on the porch at the same time) and bought
a new, first year Toyota Celica "ST" with a 1.9 liter
engine and a twin SU downdraft Carb. It was quite
the come down from my beautiful stingray, but she
was a gas guzzling mother and the little red semi-
sports car was far more practical. Celicas were new
to the world, looked sporty and refreshing, and had
Toyota dependability. I figured I'd need that kind
of reliability and gas mileage if I was to become a

road warrior. I then
resigned from my
job at the hospital,
and told my parents
that I was heading
to Florida for a "few
weeks." It was a
dead give away when I crammed every last one of my
personal possessions in the car. And to my parent's sad
remembrance, I never came home to live again.

ccccAs I arrived in Lauderdale for the first time, I was
greeted with sunny skies and summer-like weather in
the middle of snowy January. It didn't take a genius
to figure out that this was a paradise of sorts, and I
was instantly motivated to become a native. Dan
had a one bedroom apartment in south Lauderdale,
and had given instructions on where to find the spare
key. After stowing my essentials and throwing on a
pair of trunks, I headed to the beach to look him up.
His shop was a well-known retail establishment and
not hard to find. There he was, working the beach in

his red Speedo (I can't believe we wore those things!)
renting umbrellas, chairs and catamarans. We enthu-
siastically hugged and after a few minutes of orien-
tation, I was draped in a beach chair, slathering on
suntan lotion, drinking in the gorgeous ocean, its
fabulous beach, and very curvy inhabitants!

Over the next week, Dan and I talked about me
returning to school somewhere down there, but we
hatched a plan for me to find some work in the meantime and make my visit more permanent. I had to
find some sort of job anyway as I had a modest car
payment and my reserves wouldn't hold out for long.
With an agreement that I could share the rent and
claim the couch, I started looking for employment.
Having a five-year hospital background, I moseyed
over to Holy Cross, the area's largest medical center,
and applied for work. The director of the Pharmacy/
Central Services called me in for an interview and
within a week I was a Holy Cross pharmacy techni-
cian. Within six months, I had weaseled my way into
a management job as the director of Central Services
department (that's a story for another time), and with
the purchase of a Florida license tag, I had become an
official snow bird.

Meanwhile, Dan and I accommodated the revolv-
ing door of visitors at the apartment, every family
member, friend, partial-friend, and a few total strangers from Baltimore who wanted to vacation in sunny
FLA. The eight hundred square feet was no match for
the cheapskates who did the hotel head-fake and with

no coaxing or invitation agreed to stay at our place. I guess it was reverse justice for all of those years we bummed and slummed with the girls at Ocean City. However, when one particular girl came for a week's visit, Cupid's arrow found Dan's heart. The result was terminal and six months later, he was living back in Baltimore, preparing to marry a beautiful girl named Kippie!

With the apartment now mine, I settled into my new life as a hotshot hospital manager, lab coat and all! Throw in the beach, the ocean, great friends and a vigorous dating life, and I was a happy man. Meanwhile, my own thoughts of returning to school waned badly in the midst of this vibrant adventure. And as if to accent the excitement, there were the fabulous cars of the "Gold Coast!" Lauderdale offered a feast of exotic vehicles driven by well-heeled owners. For the gearhead, rubber necking became a mandatory exercise. And when a single guy could date a cute nurse AND enjoy her great car, it was a match made in heaven. I dated one girl for a number of weeks who owned a very cool gun-metal grey 1971 124 Fiat Spider convertible with red interior, which she graciously let me drive on every outing. Another gal, a nurse from ICU, owned a '71 454 Malibu Super Sport, a car she actually wanted to trade me, dead-even, for my measly Celica. I was SO close to that deal, but we broke off our relationship. It would have been rather awkward asking, "Yeah, but can I still have your car?"

Then I met this fellow, Paul. He was a six foot, four inch sheet metal worker, married to a nurse whom I befriended, and they lived a most fascinating life. Paul and his wife Alethea were twenty years older and for some reason took me in as if I were their lost son. During my first dinner at their home, I discovered Paul was a very bright, even brilliant guy; an inventor and master fabricator, who had cleverly designed and professionally finished inventions all over their house. During the day he carried a union card and worked construction to pay the bills, but at night he'd work in his shop cobbling together usable gadgets, tools and appliances, and then would file patents on them when he was satisfied he had cornered a market. He was a blue-blood of sorts, originating from a prominent Florida family, and his brother was the chairman of one of Wall Street's most prestigious brokerage firms. Paul was every bit as savvy, but he and his nurse wife marched to a different drum. Let's just say they were the family's black sheep, and they proudly wore the label, wanting nothing to do with high society or its associated snobbery. As if to add to his mystique, he was a major motorcycle freak. He held some sort of Daytona Beach land world speed record on a pan-head Harley. He lived to ride, and we became tremendous friends.

In between my many other activities, he talked me into buying a Yamaha dirt bike so that we could ride on weekends. Since I was a beginner and my only motorcycle experience was Doug's treacherous Honda 50, he encouraged me towards a 175 Yamaha Enduro, and I cut my teeth riding that bike at every possible opportunity, even using it as my daily com-

muter. And to my friend's amusement, its garage was my living room! Within months, my riding skills grew, and we had graduated to serious trail riding.

With Paul's help, I had bored and stroked the engine, added an expansion chamber, replaced the rear tire with a huge "knobby," raised the front fender, and replaced the handlebars with competition endure bars. My little two stroke, one lung Yamaha-ha-ha would flat scat!

Trail riding in Florida takes some practice because most every path is sand, and until you've driven a motorcycle in powdery sugar, you can't appreciate how difficult it is (but still not as hard as riding in streetcar tracks!). But in my attempt to keep up with a pro, I learned to handle the hardest terrains. It's not "if" you go down on a motorcycle; it's "when!" I had laid down the 175 several times during my experiences. It just happens when sand riding. But I hadn't taken any serious falls. Paul and I rode almost every weekend and with each successive adventure, we pushed the envelope further.

On one memorable occasion, we were with two other guys and flying through the woods on a snake like trail. I made the split decision to leave the trail and cut through the undergrowth where I'd emerge back on the trail and ahead of my companions. I was running through tall grass at about 30 m.p.h. when my front wheel struck a six inch tall tree stump. It was enough to send the bike end over end, flipping me over the handlebars and back onto the path of on-coming motorcycles, one of which ran cleanly over my back! I laid there for a minute assessing the bodily damage, thinking surely I'd been mortally wounded. The others had thrown down their bikes and were rushing back to my aid. I crawled up onto my hands and knees and froze there doing more assessment, as my buddies crouched beside me, trying to read my expression. I hurt badly and the wind was knocked out of me. Surely there were ribs broken, maybe a leg or a wrist. But as the seconds passed I couldn't really determine anything broken or amiss. I finally stood, ripped off my helmet and walked in circles for a few minutes. By some miracle, I had survived a spec-tacular crash. The front wheel of my motorcycle was nicely squared off and there were a half dozen new dents and dings, but otherwise it too survived.

Later, parts of my body turned black and blue, and I experienced soreness in places I didn't know existed, but I was surprisingly not seriously injured. The joke, however, was the prefect set of tire tracks tattooed across the back of my white tee-shirt. It became a badge of honor, finding a prominent place on my living room wall, a vivid testament to my nine lives!

But I wasn't the subject of the serious accident! Paul, I, and another friend, Tom, planned a hard ride on the levees out in the Everglades, west of Daytona Beach. After weeks of anticipation, we strapped our bikes on a trailer, drove two hours north and set up camp ten miles west of the beach. Paul had years of experience riding in this part of the world and was to be our official Everglades tour guide. Early Saturday morning, we unloaded Paul's brand new Yamaha 400 four stroke, my 175 and Tom's 125 Honda. With no map, just a compass and Paul's memory, we donned our helmets and gloves, and one by one, kicked the engines to life; mine, with that expansion chamber, making the most racket! We twisted the throttles, released the clutches and shot rooster tails of sand high in the air.

It was a glorious, hot Florida morning, and we took turns passing one another along the long levees separating the swamps and the inhabitants within. The Glades are comprised of thousands of square miles of prehistoric vegetation, birds, and gators. We ran for several hours, heading deeper into the swamps, and farther from civilization. There were natural mounds and gullies (known as "whoopty-doos") over which we literally flew, catching serious air, landing on our back tires and tearing off after one another. Paul lighted out ahead of us during one long stretch and entered a ravine, deep enough to have warranted a bridge. Unfortunately, there once was a bridge there, its remains lay scattered in the gorge. Paul entered hard and fast, with intentions of zipping up and flying off the far slope, but, instead, collided with the fallen spans!

His Yamaha was no match for a pile of heavy timber and it crumbled into a heap, rocketing Paul a good distance away. We came upon the horrifying scene, seeing our friend laying at an unusual angle and the tattered remains of his new motorcycle twenty feet away. I threw my running bike down and raced into the gully, past the wreckage and up the other hill to his side. He was unconscious, and I knew we were in big trouble. These were not cell phone days, and being so deep in the Glades, they'd have been useless anyway. I had minor first aid training from the military, but most of that was lost in the Moment. I wrestled his helmet off, and checked to see if he was breathing, which he thankfully was and then, mercifully, he blinked and came to. Paul always had a great sense of humor and immediately, even in pain, said, "Hey, I'm alive!" He laid there and found it difficult to move anything, so I began checking legs and arms. He winced mightily when I moved his left leg. Our companion, Tom, and I glanced at one another with the same desperate expression, while the ever optimistic Paul asked one of us for a cigarette. We looked around knowing that we were a good twenty-five miles into the Glades, and Tom said, "I'll

stay here with him and you ride back for help!" We
agreed to the plan and off I rode, head spinning with
all the worst scenarios, chief among them, me getting
lost on the trip back!

I wasn't sure of my return route and relied on a
well-developed sense of direction and nothing else.
I'd ridden for maybe forty minutes when I came upon
what looked like an inhabited hunting cabin. My
heart leapt at its sight, and I prayed someone was
there with a phone. I slid into the dirt drive, dropped
my bike, and ran for the door, yelling for anyone to
hear. By the greatest of miracles, a rather wild eyed
older man greeted me, no doubt shocked that someone was visiting way out in the boonies. I rapidly
explained what happened and crossed my fingers that
he had a phone. "Nope," he said, "but I do have a
CB radio!" I gratefully followed him into what was
clearly a man-cave, a single large living area strewn
with fishing gear and mismatched furniture. His
CB was on the only clear spot on the rustic kitchen
counter. He set the channel for police band monitor-
ing and began radioing for help. Within minutes,
a county sheriff intercepted the call and between us
three, we triangulated our position. I wasn't sure the
old man was too happy, having his secluded fishing
lodge found, but he had a measure of compassion
and seemed genuinely eager to get Paul some help.
I agreed to head to the main road to guide whatever help we could muster back to Paul's location.

Remember, this was before hospitals had helicopters, and EMTs were simply ambulance drivers.

I thanked the gentleman and with his instructions, headed for the main highway, another fifteen minutes on a fast motorcycle. I arrived and waited for what seemed like an eternity for the first police cruiser to arrive. It was followed by an ambulance and another couple of squad cars. I described the location as best I could and said they'd have to follow me back into the Glades to reach him. I had my doubts the ambulance could make it, and they discussed calling the Air National Guard for a Helo rescue. But the driver wanted to give it a try and off we went, driving down the levees towards Paul's broken body.

By now several hours had passed, and I could only imagine the pain and shock Paul was in, or whether he was even alive. I couldn't help but believe that they thought I'd abandoned them in the swamps. We had travelled about forty-five minutes when a shocking site materialized before us. Here was Tom riding ever so slowly towards me with Paul slumped behind him on his little 125! We rushed to them, and I had never seen a more grateful face on Tom and a more agonized, whiter face on our broken friend. The ambulance drivers sprung from their vehicle, grabbed their gurney and rushed to Paul's aid. Three sheriffs hustled to Tom's bike and began helping to unload the very injured passenger.

"What happened?" I said to Tom. "Paul couldn't just lie there." Tom said. "He'd die if he didn't try to get to the main road, and he wanted to close the distance between you and him. So that's what we did!" It took another hour to get Paul to the emergency room at the Halifax General Hospital in Daytona Beach. We called his wife from the waiting room, described the gruesome ordeal, and she dropped everything and headed north. It was late afternoon when we got Paul to the hospital and well past dark when we anxiously heard news that he would survive. He had no internal injuries, but had broken a number of bones, suffered multiple contusions, and, most seriously, he had badly fractured his pelvis! Imagine him ridding on Tom's motorcycle all that way on a shattered pelvis! Eh-gads!!

Over the rest of the weekend, we enlisted his brother, Erwin's, help, and with a four by four and a trailer, we made our way back to the accident site to retrieve the remains of Paul's new Yamaha. You'd think that coming out of the military I would have had a better sense of wilderness preparedness and first aid, but I never would have thought we'd venture so far from our camp so quickly, and it caught us all by surprise. It took Paul nearly six months to recover. Meanwhile, I had doubled my cautiousness when riding, replaying the accident in my head time and again. As sobering as such events can be, it served to improve my skills and added yet another chapter in my book about life!

Chapter Twenty-Seven
SHE DROVE A BEETLE INTO MY HEART!

Four years of sunny south Florida is a lot for any-one. People, claiming they'd be permanent residents, came and went at a dizzying rate. As a hospital department manager, I hired a number of folks who vowed, "I'm in Lauderdale to stay," only to have them disappear three weeks later. Believe it or not, it was tough living in a beach town. Everyone remained in a perpetual playful mood, and serious work took a distant second place to having good time! A perfect example happened while driving to work one Mon-day morning. I was sitting at a light on A1A and a carload of seventeen somethings pulled up next to me. The entire car unloaded, everyone ran around the vehicle twice and then piled back in...a classic Chi-nese fire drill. Funny? Yes. Monday morning while I'm heading to work? No! Maybe I was actually growing up.

Surrounded by a population of transients, it was hard to make trusted friends. Paul and Alethea were real live natives, not infatuated by the beach and night life. But many around my age were there for the same reason I had journeyed south..."the sun and fun!" After four years, I had become a quasi native and was sincerely trying to make a go of it. With each passing year, there was less gravitational pull to the beach, and more focus on earning an income and getting ahead. There was certainly more motivation to return to school and to crank up my career in earnest. But I had settled into a fairly prominent manager's role in spite of a missing bachelor's degree. I came and went as I pleased, with a high degree of authority.

Even if I was maturing, I wasn't dead. Female companionship still trumped all else, including my precious cars! Therefore, a friend named Wilson, another department head, and I would make rounds at three o'clock each afternoon to check on the progress of our respective assets stationed throughout the hospital, while simultaneously assessing the nursing assets! It had become a well-known ritual and most everyone laughed at us, two single twenty-four-year-olds visiting nursing stations, making small talk and listening to the nurses giggle with, but mostly at, us!!

During those forays, I'd pass the radiation therapy department. Its door marked the beginning of a long hallway which, at the other end, sat one of the cutest

girls I had ever seen. It was maddening because I had
no Central Service products in her department; therefore, I had no legitimate excuse to "swing through."
I'd catch glimpses of this girl here and there, sometimes in the cafeteria. As I inquired about her, she
was a mystery to most of my friends, and I didn't
make much headway. I did, however, make sure she
knew I was interested, throwing her a well-timed
smile, and even locking eyes on several occasions.
This went on for seemingly weeks when one day she
showed up at my department door. How fortuitous!
"Can I help you?" I said. "I need some boxes and was
told your department had lots of empties." "Sure,
let me see what I can do...by the way, I'm Rodger" I
ventured, "And you're..." "I'm Suzanne!"she offered.
Wow, what a doll, I thought! I did my most professional box gathering and offered to help her out to her
car, to which, with a modest smile, she agreed. Geez,
the closer I got, the cuter she was, and I was busting
to ask her out. It seemed that the previous week's
smiles and glances had softened the beachhead as we
small talked out to her little green VW bug. There
was such a naturalness about inviting her to join a few
of us for a drink after work.

We met a block away and I learned that this adorable blonde, whose family had moved down from
New York, also had a long-time boy friend, Paul,
back home. But, I sensed an open door, like maybe
things weren't so peachy with her beau and that the
new guy might have a chance. So during the next

five months, our relationship blossomed from friends to quality dates, with the Paul thing lingering like an elephant in the room. But I pressed onward, taking my best swings, and Suzanne finally broke hard in my direction, lobbing Paul an official "Dear John!" grenade! In the sixth month of our relationship, I proposed to my adorable girlfriend, and she accepted.

As for a car connection with my new squeeze, there were very few during these six months. However, Suzanne discovered early that I was a car addict, and she was introduced to my madness before the first date had concluded. My Mom and Dad happened to be visiting (they had the good sense to get a hotel room) the week I had my first official date with Suz. I had asked her out to dinner with the double entrée of meeting the parents. Yes, it was kind of early to be doing that. The first date? But, hey, they were there, and I couldn't exactly avoid them. Besides, I wanted to show off this exceptionally good looking girl! Anyway, I had picked up Suzanne and brought her to my apartment before we were to meet Mom and Dad. She entered my ground floor pad for the first time, and there sat my beautiful motorcycle! "Uh, just sit anywhere around it!" Well, something like that usually is a great conversation starter... "Have ya ever ridden a motorcycle before?" I asked. "No." she said. "Would you like to?" I followed with. "Sure!" Listen, there is nothing more macho and romantic at the same time than a girl, scared to death, hugging your body, while we're screaming down the road on a pocket rocket.

So, I wheeled the thing outside and fired it off, its noise sending her hands to cover her ears. Handing her a helmet, I yelled over my shoulder for her to climb on and hold on "right here around my waist!" I kicked it into gear and tore off down the street. We'd ridden maybe three miles, imparting the thrill and enjoying the exciting closeness when I saw the all too familiar blue lights flashing in my mirror. Holy crap, I was being pulled over!! I was only a block from my apartment when I moved to the curb, killed the engine, threw down the kickstand, and dismounted (trying not to kick Suzanne in the face as I swung my leg over the tank!).

How utterly embarrassing! I recall walking back to the cruiser, asking Suz to just stay put, and remember the funny image of her sitting there, back to me, cocked at an angle because the bike was leaning on its stand, and thinking, "if this doesn't run her off, nothing will!!" Well, I presented the policeman with my license, and he returned to his car to check me out. I had sauntered back to her and was attempting to explain that it was probably just a routine stop or my muffler was too loud, something minor I'm sure, when three other police cruisers descended on us and hemmed us in. The original cop approached me as the others were climbing out of their cars. I was thinking, "What in the …?" "Son, we have your bike listed as stolen! May I see your registration?" he said sternly. "What?" Stolen?" "No, I don't have my registration, but I live right there and can get it for you!" Now I'm mortified and positive Suzanne was thinking, "Who is this thieving creep and what have I gotten myself into?" I had them follow me to my apartment where I produced ample documentation proving that I wasn't John Dillinger. With the drama behind us, I wheeled the bike back into the living room and spent the next hour apologizing for that horrible experience. I knew she liked me when she laughed it off. At week's end, when the parents were leaving, Mom remarked to my father, "He's gonna marry that girl!"

We did, exactly one year later. But it, too, wasn't without drama. Remember the last scene in the movie, "The Graduate"? Benjamin Braddock, played by Dustin Hoffman, screams Elaine Robinson's name, played by Katharine Ross, over and over as she is about to marry Carl. She turns and runs to Ben and mayhem breaks out! Well, ex-boyfriend Paul was among the New York friends invited to the ceremony, and they had to restrain a very drunken version of him in the back of the church, something thankfully neither of us knew took place until after the wedding. It could have been a real-life movie scene! Would she have said, "I'm coming, Paul!"…nah!

Okay, so what did this have to do with cars? Obviously not much! Our first official joint signing act, though, was the purchase of a beautiful blue 1975 Celica "GT" with white interior, loaded to the teeth. I still remember driving off of the Toyota lot with its factory in-dash stereo blaring "One of These Nights" by the Eagles. But, honestly, I didn't spend a lot of time thinking about my wheels during that year. Instead, I was, and still am, madly in love with my Suzanne!

Chapter Twenty-Eight
MY FIRST PORSCHE

I married that sweet girl thirty-six years ago! After the wedding we settled into a tiny apartment near the beach and learned to be married for a year. I was pretty much relegated to *Hot Rod* and *Car and Driver* magazines to fulfill my car fantasizes since covering our combined bills was making short work of our two incomes. While at Holy Cross I was introduced to a hospital management corporation named ServiceMaster for whom my friend Wilson worked. SM was contracted to manage several departments within our medical center. Seeing an opportunity to advance, I was courted and hired by them and after eight weeks of training, I was transferred to my first assignment, Parkridge Hospital in Chattanooga, Tennessee. Suz and I loaded up her green VW and my Celica, kissed the family and friends good bye, dropped the clutches, and headed north.

After several years in the Scenic City, a sizable promotion was offered, which meant moving to the

SM home office in Chicago. But Suz and I loved our little town and, instead, elected to stay put by buying our first business, a ServiceMaster janitorial "franchise." My company offered a division where this was possible. I had wanted to try my hand at business ownership from childhood. Dad had toyed with being in his own business fifty times over, always showing us the next great scheme that would launch the Piersants into financial independence. But he could never afford to leave his good paying job. So, like him, we could either stay in the corporate life or take the plunge while we had nothing to lose. We chose the latter. My hospital counterparts thought we'd lost our minds at the announcement of our decision. I even remember thinking, "Are we doing the right thing?" But we dove in and began our life of entrepreneurism.

Suz and I worked pretty much day and night that first year, me selling all day, and, then with a handful of new employees, cleaning those hard-fought-for few banks and offices. I remember with fondness my wife's dedication, vacuuming a bank at ten o'clock at night while nine months pregnant. And I recall being decked out in my ServiceMaster blazer and tie, visiting a customer one morning to inquire about our performance, only to discover we had missed emptying several trash cans the night before...an account I had cleaned myself! I assured the customer I'd have a talk with THAT employee! But slowly we added new contracts, and like a phoenix rising, the business blossomed. By year's end, we had fourteen building contracts and twenty-eight people working with us. We were exhausted but happy and truly in business for ourselves!

By our fourth year (1980), we had landed over forty building contracts and had seventy or so people working for us. Now Suzanne was able to work out of the house, loving and mothering our two-year-old, while meticulously keeping our books! And with a growing discretionary income, I was able to purchase my first 911 Porsche. It was a white "T" model. Since my rides in Mr. Cohen's 356, I had my heart set on owning one. I spotted her sitting at a European mechanic's shop while traveling between accounts, and, like gravity, was almost pulled into the parking lot by an immediate emotional attachment. Its owner had just dumped nine grand on the motor and needed out from under the car before the bill came due. The body was straight, the black interior was excellent and, as expected, it ran excep-tionally well with the help of new every-thing. I wheeled it out on a test drive and, being my first 911 experience, I was not sure what to expect. But the German-born mechanic rode along and gave me a minute by minute lesson in authentic broken English on every noise, feel and sensation the Porsche threw off. He schooled me on the virtues and down-falls of the 911breed and invited me to push it to its performance envelope to prove his points. Although the "T" was the weakest 911@ 125 horse from its 2.2 liter engine, compared to its fuel injected 175 horse brother, the "E," and most powerful 180 horse "S," he had converted the Zenith carbs to Webers, added Carrera chain tensioners and a few other goodies, and the Porsche was a lot livelier than I expected. It wasn't my Corvette by any means, but you could feel its thoroughbred pedigree and knew it was born to race.

I negotiated a sweet deal with the guy and drove my 911 home. Not being satisfied with the paint nor with the least expensive steel wheels, I took it to a body man for a full makeover, even changing its paint color to beautiful Porsche Red. I then found a set of cookie cutter alloy wheels and shod the sports car with decent Michelins. When done, it was rather stunning looking, a refreshed Porsche with a grossly expensive new engine. I knew it wasn't the class of the field, but it was MY first Porsche, and I was going to savor it.

It ran beautifully and driving it daily was a hoot, even though it had some spirited rear-engine handling quirks. If you own a Porsche, you need to be prepared to own a Porsche. By that I mean they are fabulous cars that can be fabulously expensive to repair. So, one becomes quite handy at the minor repairs. After six months, I determined that I needed a second gear synchronizer. Before returning to the mechanic from whom I bought the car, I had been told about the singing Vickery brothers, two boys who were perhaps the finest Porsche mechanics in the

Southeast, with an equal amount of musical talent. They had built an enormous Porsche/BMW repair shop in Atlanta, and, for family reasons, moved to Chattanooga and restarted their business. Waymon, the older brother, was the Porsche guy, and by last count had owned thirty eight 911s, including some truly exotic twin turbos. He also had a wonderful singing voice and actually took guitar lesson from Chet Akins! We're talking high cotton here!

When I went to pick up the car, he said, "I can make that car a lot faster!" "How?' I asked. "Let me tune it," he said. Believing the press on these guys, I let him at it and returned the next day. Waymon was and remains one of the truly under-spoken men of our time. "I think you'll find her a little quicker!" he said. I climbed in and started it and immediately recognized a freer throttle response. Through the open window I said, "What did you do?" "Your carburetors were all out of whack. She'll run good now!" I settled up with Mr. Vickery, jumped back in the car and headed down their driveway to the major thoroughfare. I then eased into traffic and ran up through the gears, noticing not only my tranny shifting effortlessly, but the revs rushing freely between gears. "Are you kidding me?" I thought. I edged over to the fast lane, brought it back into second, and jumped on it hard. I had redlined to third and fourth before letting off of it, and I determined that the Vickery brothers must have been magicians as well!

Chapter Twenty-Nine
MY TWO FAVORITE CARS!

I've enjoyed plenty of sweet rides during the past thirty-five years! And my brother certainly has! He has lived in southern California the majority of these years, but we've never failed to check in and out of habit, we start our conversations with, "So, what are you driving?" Between Doug and I, we've owned three 911s; one 356 Carrera; three Corvettes including a Z06; one streetrod; three Audis; one Ferrari, three Mercedes; one 427 Cobra; two Nissan "Z"s; one Shelby Mustang; one Roush 427 Mustang; one Ford Lightening; two Hemi Dodges; three motorcycles; and one twin turbo BMW. And that's not counting our wives cars, many of which were pretty cool too!

In the mid '80s, I decided I'd like to try my hand at street rodding. I'd travel to all the hot rod shows and weekend affairs, buy *Rodder* Magazines, and generally stay in touch with hot rodding trends and fashions. While at a local show one weekend, I found a 1923 Ford T-Bucket that had been built in the mid '60s and was needing some serious attention and a new owner. I figured I should start with something simple, and there's nothing simpler than a "Bucket." Its owner and I haggled for a few minutes, and having won a decent price, I drove the radical "T" home. Our then twelve-and ten-year-old sons were amazed, shocked and delighted. "What are we going to do with it, Dad?" they asked. "I'm going to rebuild it just the way I want it!" I told them.

And then the real work began. I made plans and drawings for how the car would look, poured over magazines and cut out various pictures, lived in parts catalogs, made lists and would sit staring at it, visualizing the end result. Over the next year, I dismantled the car to the frame, storing and categorizing nuts, bolts, seats, gauges, engine goodies, wiring... you name it. And I threw out as much as I stored! My garage had morphed into an auto parts warehouse and to the untrained eye, my wife's in particular, it looked like a bomb had exploded. I, however, knew where everything was...kind of.

Anyway, the project started taking shape when I found the right guys to sandblast the frame. The car originally had a metal flake green colored body with black roll and tufted interior and a black frame, typical of the early '60s rodding styles. Once back from the shop, I was ready for body work and paint. I had befriended a hotrod builder who recommended some quality paint guys, so I loaded up the collective parts and headed their way. I had decided on a black and yellow paint scheme, and although the black was easy to code and spray, I wanted the yellow to be startling. My idea was to have the car completely yellow from the front axle and radiator housing back through the engine rails, up the firewall and to the windshield. And from the windshield back, the yellow would fade into red flames and then deep gloss black, all transitioning at the doors.

In my search for the perfect yellow, I found an outrageous yellow '40 Ford in one of my magazines. Its owner was named in the article and lived across the country in L.A. With the operator's help, I dialed eight or nine people before I found the right guy, who gladly shared the color PPG 2988 1977 Corvette yellow, the only yellow with a yellow base, not green. With weeks of prep and taping off the flames on the body, we shot the yellow and then reversed the process and shot the black. In the end I picked up a fabulous looking hand rubbed body and frame. I then sent the interior out to another local rod builder who did a killer makeover using bright red leather, picking up the red tipped flames on the doors.

Okay, what about the power, you say? That was the best part. The engine was a four bolt main 350 Chevy bored over .33 to make it a stroker motor, flat top pistons, a 400 crank and a 292 Competition cam, a highrise manifold, ported and polished intakes, and a polished Holley 780 duel-feed. The power was put to the ground through a Turbo 400 and a 10 inch Ford rear with 3.90 gears. I painted the block a matching yellow, and dressed it in gobs of polished stainless, from alternators to headers, to complete the transformation. Over the next year, I pieced the car back together, adding touches like Autometer gauges, a way cool air intake, matching wiring, huge rear Mickey Thompson tires, skinny front drag tires and exceptional looking custom Weld wheels all four corners. The Hurst shifter was topped off with a matching yellow Mooneyed cueball. Finally, I hired one of the South's best pin-striper to outline my flames in baby blue, to throw some crazy wild designs on my front spring clamp, and, for good measure, the rear-end housing.

The car tipped the scales at just over 1,100 pounds and with horsepower well north of 450, it was outrageously quick and "Rat Fink" scary. Admittedly, T-Buckets can look out of proportion, amateurish, or just plain cheap. But for guys who lived in the Big Daddy Roth era, we know what Ts are supposed to look like. Mine was a one-car parade. I eventually sold it to Corky Coker, the Vintage tire mogul, and it rests in his car collection. It was great fun and was usually the buzz at the auto shows. Of course, there were some serious rods in our town; great '32s and '33s, lots of lead sleds, and several great $100,000 plus creations. Mine was just a beginner's streetrod with a professional touch, but, in the hotrod world, it's always "your" creation, and that's enough!

As much as I loved that hotrod, my most all time valued car was bought from my friend, Waymon. As I said, he had owned many Porsche 911s, but his favorite, in his recollection, was mine as well. It was a 1984 Porsche Carrera with a special pedigree. Waymon was a good friend of Peter Shutz, the then president of Porsche, and under Peter's and his own supervision, had this car built. Waymon lived in Germany during the month of its construction and reported to the Stuttgart plant everyday. I have the original pictures as it developed through various stages of hand fabrication. When competed, its 1984 window sticker listed the price at $37,628, 90% more than a new 1984 Corvette! My friend brought it home from Germany and after just 5,000 miles and fanatical persuasion from his family doctor, sold it to his doc, in whose hands and garage it remained

until I wrestled it away a few years later. The car was a gorgeous zinc metallic color with blue leather interior, Fuch wheels, limited slip differential, titanium bolts in the engine, heated and tinted windshield, Blaupunkt sound system and the Carrera whale tail! And, of course, it was perfect and classically beautiful.

In the mid '70s, Porsche went through a crisis of sorts, building 911s with engines that would have catastrophic failures at around 50,000 miles. This was because the '74 through '77 models sported an increased displacement 2.7 liter motor, using the older 2.4 engine and in the transformation, the thermal studs in the aluminum heads would pull away from the crank case as they expanded and contracted from heat, dumping volumes of oil in the process. In 1978, the problem was remedied with an all new "bulletproof" 3 liter engine, which produced 188 horses. By 1984 the displacement had raised to 3.2 liters, and with the addition of Motronic electronic fuel injection and self oiling chain tensioners, it was a fabulous motor. In its American dress, it produced 207 b.h.p. a 149 m.p.h. top speed and 0-60 times of 5.6 seconds, but mine was a German version at 231 h.p. The car weighed in at just 2,760 pounds and was super quick and super fun. Many Porsche-philes believe that '84 through '89 were the best sequence of improving years for Porsche, '84 being simply tremendous, '86 being even better with the G50 transmission, and the '89 begin the best of the lot, the last year before mass production took over. I couldn't have agreed more.

I happily drove my Porsche for many years, enjoying the rush and sound of its flat six, and the precision and quality in every aspect of its being. The doors closed like vaults and the no-nonsense instrument cluster, with the large faced tach front and center, made it a thrilling automobile to own and drive. I bought the car with just a few miles on it and sold it in 2007 with just over 50,000 miles. I sadly waved goodbye when the owner of a Porsche dealership in Pennsylvania made me an offer I couldn't refuse. I would have kept it forever, but with low mileage on a 1984 car of its caliber, it had reached its zenith in pricing, and I had to let it go. And my philosophy in life, about cars, and all else is simple…try not to let good things ever become ultimate things!

These two cars were but a few of the toys I've enjoyed amidst a most blessed life. I'd like to share that which gave my life meaning and is best summarized in this book's epilogue.

Epilogue
THE PARADE OF PROVIDENCE!

Lest you think me a completely shallow twit, babbling on about my cars, I did discover that cars for me are a wonderful hobby. But life is to be lived with purpose and meaning. All of my cars were buried in a history of life lived among the people I love. Our sons grew, finished college, married, and now we enjoy the significant privilege of loving our two granddaughters, one grandchild on the way as this writing, and one granddog! Vocationally, Service-Master led to the opportunity to help start and grow a national nonprofit organization dedicated to helping kids on school campuses cope with a host of life controlling issues. At last count, and under the leadership of a great friend, National Center for Youth Issues is serving 23,000 schools and school systems! For almost twelve years, I served as its first president and that position morphed into a consulting role for several of the nation's larger private foundations.

This led to purchasing a manufacturing company with several partners. We're starting our twelfth year of making displays and fixtures for the retail industry serving such clients as Lowes, Home Depot, Crystal Water, and Mohawk Flooring. Throughout the decades of thick and thin, Suzanne and I have learned what Don Henley sings, "to want what we have and take what we are given with grace!" Like most adults, we began to make sense of our lives not in a moment but in an unfolding story of extraordinary opportunities mixed with equally thorny challenges.

From 1981 forward, our lives took an interesting turn. Our second son, Timothy, was born. I returned to college and was awarded with that forever discussed bachelors degree, and even went on to finish grad school. Our business was expanding, and winning awards for growth and service. From 1981 through 1984 we racked up quite a few pieces of hardware and accolades from our parent company thanks to over one hundred and ten long term contracts and employing 255 people in three Tennessee cities. We were cleaning universities, government buildings, banks, and tourist attractions. I bought a new white Audi 5000 and drove it hard and often. That car and I became good friends! And it was followed with a new Mercedes as well as a 280Z 2+2. And if these material benchmarks weren't enough, in 1984 we were notified that we had been awarded the top prize, the Marion E. Wade trophy, named after our founder and given to the number one business of our 3,600 counterparts worldwide. It was like winning the Super Bowl and a memorable time for my wife and me. Here I was thirty four years old and at the top of my game.

What do you do for an encore when you've reached your goals? It just so happened that I had experienced a life changing event three years prior, and decisions and concern about our future were given some perspective.

I was sitting at my desk when a friend from a neighboring Knoxville franchise came visiting. His name was Bill. He was an older gentleman with a sweet demeanor and a well established business. He was easy to be friends with and seemed genuinely interested in me and our business. Bill sat across my desk and perceived a restlessness in me born from my ambition and the strain of a large and rapidly growing company. "What's important to you, Rodge?" he asked. "I dunno know...certainly family, this business, maybe cars and music, I'm not really sure beyond those," I replied. "What's your ultimate goal?" he followed with. "Geezz, Bill, I guess security, good health....enough money to retire?" I ventured. "Nah...those aren't good enough," he said. "You really don't know what you want, do ya?" he said bluntly but with a smile. "I guess not," I replied with some resignation. Bill was staring at an upwardly mobile young man with lots of potential, material trappings, and an empty future. The most that could be said was I was a pretty nice guy, and maybe not even that.

"So, where's this going?" I asked Bill. "Well, Rodge," he started, "I was once where you were, and found out quickly that more is never enough. What's your faith life like?" he asked. "What do ya mean, Bill, my church life?" I asked. "Yes and no," he said. "A whole bunch of us attend church, but that doesn't mean you love God any more than a sitting in a doctor's office makes you a doctor!" he quipped. "Do you have faith?" he continued. "I believe there's a God," I said, now getting a little uncomfortable. The fact was, I had encountered God as an adult in the midst of my days in Fort Lauderdale and was sensitive to His presence, but had not given definition to those beliefs. Besides this, I only had the remnants of a childhood church life. So, what did I believe? What were my ultimate goals? Was building a business and making money the actualization of my existence?

Bill, sensing my discomfort broke off the line of questioning and said, "Ya know, Rodge, you need to meet a friend of mine who lives right here in Chattanooga. His name is Roger too, he has a heck of a business mind, and he might consider mentoring you."

Two weeks later, I found myself sitting in this other Roger's office. He was the Executive Vice President of an organization called the Christian Business Men's Committee. He had left a lucrative insurance business to serve in this role. "So, Bill tells

me you have a growing franchise!" he started. "It's
pretty good," I said with some modest pride. "Where
do you think it will take you?" he said. "Wow, you
guys ask some tough questions!" I replied. He smiled
and said, "Let me ask you, what's your relationship
like with God?" Now I was starting to believe that
he and Bill were part of some some crazy Christian
cult or clandestine society complete with a secret
handshake. "Rog, Bill asked me the same question.
I believe there's a God and I attend a church with
my wife and kids. What does that have to do with
anything?" I pressed. Rog wouldn't be put off that
easily. He said, "Well, would you like to meet once a
week, and we can talk how your business is integrated
with faith?" It certainly sounded intriguing, and I
agreed to meet with him the following week. "Oh,
and bring a Bible," he said. "Great!" I thought, "Do
I even have a Bible?"

The following week we met at his office, me lugging a big old family Bible, and we sat at a small
round table in the corner of his office. He handed me
three books called *Operation Timothy* and explained
that we'd be going through this together, book by
book, chapter by chapter. Rog asked if he could pray
for us before we began. I looked around and uncom-
fortably said yes, and off he started, praying for me,
us, our future and what I was about to learn. I'm not
sure I had ever been prayed for in such a personal
manner. And I wasn't sure I had ever heard anyone
with authenticity, peace and grace, praying to God in

such a personal way. I was humbled, and he had my attention!

Over a three month period, Rog and I faithfully met, me studying my Bible and sifting through the questions in the Timothy Study, and then the two of us working together to understand the meaning of life and my life as it was meant to be lived. Through each question, Rog patiently guided and instructed me until I began to see for myself God's purposes for my life. Each revelation quickened my heart, and the truth of my vacant condition and the futility of my worldly striving unfolded before me.

I arrived at the understanding that I was not the center of my universe and I grew into a deep and abiding relationship with God. I discovered that there was a great, uncrossable chasm between Him and me, formed when our man, Adam, first sinned, dooming all of mankind. But God, the Father, who first and always loved us, desired reconciliation and put into motion a plan to redeem me and all creation back to Himself, culminating in the sacrifice of His only Son as a lasting payment for my rebellion. I simply had to recognize and confess that I, too, was God's enemy, and believe that Christ hung on that cross in my place. As the notion of my self indulgence, aggrandizement, and eventual permanent separation from Him sank in, I longed for His rescue and received it in a moment of prayerful surrender at Rog's corner desk.

Now after all of these years, I have experienced mercy for my sins, grace for my future ones and peace in what is otherwise a rat-race culture! I've grown to see Him as the object of my ultimate affection, recognizing His rightful authority and dominion over all things, including my family, my vocation, and even my cars. I receive my daily portion, sometimes humbly and sometimes kicking and screaming as the "Adam-ic" nature still lives in this old boy. But perhaps best of all, in spite of my sometimes bad behavior, God now sees His own son when He looks at me. When it finally sunk in that the Creator of the universe loved me that much, my life changed, and so can yours. I don't care who you are or what you've done, God's promise holds true for you too.

That is why when we were at the top of our business game, I realized that it wasn't about the money, the fame or the trappings. These things were fine, kept in perspective, but if they became my idols, then God wasn't. "No man can serve two masters. He'll either hate the one or love the other, or be devoted to one and despise the other. No man can serve God and money!" (Matthew 6:24). You can't go wrong with a God whose first command is to Love Him with all of your heart, soul, and mind and to love others as yourself! (Matthew 22:37). You may also be saying, "We're way off the reservation here! This car book has ended in a Dad-gum sermon! Fine, I get it! But, I didn't want to leave you with an impression that my life is about cars. It's far from it. And when you've come to the end of yourself or your life or your loved one's life and nothing makes sense, you may wish you knew the Creator. I'd love to talk cars with you and even more so, would love to share the secret to a fulfilled life. Contact me at rpiersant@comcast.net, and we'll make a date to chat.

So, do I still love my cars? You bet! They are a great source of enjoyment and part of my DNA. I love my music, too. It is a gift I exercise as often as I can. I'm crazy about my family, the jewel in my crown, and, of course you've just heard, I love my God, deeply! Thanks for sharing in my life and my passions, and in this case, my appetite for the automobile. You can see I'm "working my addiction steps," with my Higher Power in mind. It has minimized my insatiable need for sheet metal and tires. Just maybe your MAO can be cured too!!

Acknowledgments

Although many of these images and thoughts were derived from fifty-nine years of life, I needed lots of help to form this into some sort of readable manuscript. A special thanks to Jenny Sanders for her love of English and grammar, which I can trash in a New York minute. Thanks to Bob Tamasy, my real author friend, who read it and deemed it readable! I have to recognize the hard work from editors and writers of many issues of *Motor Trend*, *Car and Driver*, *Hot Rod*, *Rodder*, and *Road and Track Magazines*. I also want to thank Randy Leffingwell and Jim Campisano for their many car books, which both reminded me and taught me new facts about many of the cars in my life. I am not ashamed to say that even Wikipedia was a big help and deserves my gratitude. A special thanks to Mark Cubberly for the use of his beautiful Superformance Cobra in the cover photo. Watch out, Mark, that car may become mine! A very special thanks to Joe Novenson and Gary Purdy, two great friends and pastors who have helped me have joy in following Christ. Mostly, I want to thank my precious wife, my brother Doug and sister Cheryl, and my entire family for putting up with me all of these years. And for my 91 year old Mom, I am so sorry for the many times I broke your heart, or hid these things from you. I'm most thankful to God that you have lived long for these antics to become distant, even funny memories. I love you!

Made in the USA
Charleston, SC
09 February 2017